Everyday People, Everyday Grace

Daily Meditations
for Busy Christians

George R. Szews

ACTA
Assisting Christians To Act
PUBLICATIONS

Everyday People, Everyday Grace
Daily Meditations for Busy Christians
by George R. Szews

Rev. George Szews is a priest of the Diocese of La Cross, Wisconsin. He is the author of the *Why I Am Catholic: 21 People Give Their Own Reasons* and the co-author of *Between Now and Forever: Planning the Catholic Funeral*, both published by ACTA Publications.

"My gratitude to the everyday people of the Newman Parish in Eau Claire, Wisconsin who have encouraged me to write these stories; to Flo Sheridan who lent a patiently kind but not uncritical eye to the manuscript; to Michael Joncas who reminds me everyday grace is not as hidden as I sometimes think; and to my parents, Rupert and Genevive Szews, who first taught me that loving a good story and loving God are nearly–but not exactly–the same thing." – George R. Szews

Edited by Francine O'Connor
Cover design by Tom A. Wright
Design and Typesetting by Garrison Publications

Published by: ACTA Publications
                Assisting Christians To Act
                4848 N. Clark Street
                Chicago, IL 60640
                773-271-1030

Library of Congress Catalog Number: 97-74029
ISBN: 0-87946-166-7
Printed in the United States of America
01 00 99 98   5 4 3 2

Chosen

He wanted to believe the note she wrote in the card: "Forget the past. It's gone now, like leaves withered in the snow. Look to the future. You will find God there making you new and strong, healing your brokenness."

He wondered if it was that easy, if the turn of a calendar page made all the difference, and if God who had been around so long could possibly care about one more son of Adam.

Luke 12:6

> "Are not five sparrows sold for two pennies? Yet not one of them is forgotten in God's sight. But even the hairs of your head are all counted. Do not be afraid; you are of more value than many sparrows."

Born to Righteousness

The stranger picked up the dollar bill that dropped from her pocket and ran after her to return it. As he placed it in her hand, she held it by the tiniest tip, afraid that whatever germs this obvious street person might have had on his hands would infect her. She thanked him with a sweet smile, waited until he was around the corner, then threw the dollar bill into the trash can outside the grocery store.

1 John 2:29

If you know that [Jesus] is righteous, you may be sure that everyone who does right has been born of him.

Becoming Jesus

The boy was only about two feet tall then, with a shock of blond hair that defied slicking down. Tugging at the priest's vestments until he had all of his attention, he would say, "Hi Jesus!" Then he'd run off, laughing and proud, to catch up with his mother.

The boy grew up and stopped coming to church altogether. One day he ran into his pastor on the street. He would have walked right by him if the priest hadn't called out his name. As they stood there making small talk, the priest remembered the small boy tugging again at his vestments with a secret to tell.

The young man began to walk away, then turned and shouted, "Hey. Keep the faith!"

"Always." The priest yelled back. "You, too!"

The young man laughed. "I got to," he said, "I used to know Jesus."

"Maybe it's your turn to be Jesus," the priest yelled into the wind.

John 13:20

> "Very truly, I tell you, whoever receives one whom I send receives me; and whoever receives me receives him who sent me."

True Reflections

She loved to travel for work and stay in hotels where no one cares how much water you use in the tub. At home, she didn't have enough money to fix the water heater, which warmed just enough tepid water for a quick shower. But she did not like the full-length mirrors that usually cover the bathroom walls in most hotels.

On one trip, she asked for extra sheets and tucked them over the corners of the mirror. She didn't want to see herself coming out of the tub. She could not deal with how she had aged and how imperfect her body had become.

A friend asked to use her bathroom that night before the evening conference. Coming out of the bathroom, her friend asked about the sheets hung over the mirror.

"Oh that," the woman said. "I don't want God to see me without my makeup."

---

1 John 3:2

Beloved, we are God's children now; what we will be has not yet been revealed. What we do know is this: when he is revealed, we will be like him, for we will see him as he is.

BE IT RESOLVED

By January fifth, he had lost his list of new year's resolutions. He couldn't even remember what they were.

1 JOHN 3:18

Little children, let us love, not in word or speech, but in truth and action.

THE LIGHT

The boy hated winter; it was always dark when he came home from school. Every afternoon, as he turned onto his street, he would look for the porch light, which was always on for his return. Then he would set his course and almost fly the rest of the way home. He could almost smell dinner cooking on the stove when he hit that corner.

LUKE 11:36

"If then your whole body is full of light, with no part of it in darkness, it will be as full of light as when a lamp gives you light with its rays."

DIALING DIRECT

She usually found it easier to pray for strangers, about whom she knew nothing, than to pray for the things she needed herself.

1 JOHN 5:14-15

And this is the boldness we have in him, that if we ask anything according to his will, he hears us. And if we know that he hears us in whatever we ask, we know that we have obtained the requests made of him.

LEFTOVER LOVE

He finally hauled the Christmas tree to the collection area where the city would chip it up and give it away in the spring as mulch. As he was leaving, he noticed several poor children run up to the stack of trees to search for ornaments inadvertently left behind or forgotten bits of tinsel. "Get away from there," he shouted. "Those trees don't belong to you!"

1 JOHN 3:17

How does God's love abide in anyone who has the world's goods and sees a brother or sister in need and yet refuses help?

GOD'S LOVE

Her parents had taken care to nurture her self-esteem. She had no doubt that God loved her, but she found it hard to believe that God loved everyone else equally. How could she be special if God loved others as much as God loved her?

1 JOHN 4:11-12

Beloved, since God loved us so much, we also ought to love one another. No one has ever seen God; if we love one another, God lives in us and his love is perfected in us.

TROUBLE

The question might have sounded more sincere had it not been shouted across the street: "Did you get in trouble?" The answer, driven against a strong wind, lost its true emotional context: "Yea!"

"How big a trouble?" came the next question. "Big."

"Bigger than when you tied your cat's tail to your little sister's stroller?" "Yea!"

"Bigger than when you poured a bottle of glue down the bathroom sink?" "Yea!"

"Bigger than when you burned down the dog house?" "Yea!"

"Now *that's* trouble!"

The wave each gave to the other had enough spirit to raise a smile and enough sadness to cultivate the realization that the older you get the bigger the trouble.

1 JOHN 5:3-4

For the love of God is this, that we obey his commandments. And his commandments are not burdensome, for whatever is born of God conquers the world.

KING AND CONQUEROR

They were in sixth grade the year it snowed every other day. The street crew had plowed huge mounds of snow into their playground. Boys and girls together joined in the rough and tumble sport of shoving each other off the mountain. It came as a shock to the boys when the girls banded together, shoved every one of them off the mountain, and declared a corporate kingship. The boys knew that only the strong could be king, and they began hurling insults instead of snowballs.

That afternoon, the principal announced that king of the mountain was now banned. It would take them a lifetime to learn that this was for the good of their souls and not the care of their bodies.

1 JOHN 5:5

Who is it that conquers the world
but the one who believes that Jesus
is the Son of God?

DISCERNMENT

Looking through the business directory in the phone book under "churches," she was amazed by the number, but even more so by the variety. Some proclaimed programs and services to enhance her personal growth. Others simply stated they existed. How does one choose?

1 JOHN 5:20

And we know that the Son of God has come and has given us understanding so that we may know him who is true.

Keeping Up

Flipping through a magazine, he was convinced that he needed the three thousand dollar watch displayed in the four-color, full-page ad. After all, the fifty-nine dollar watch he was convinced he needed a couple of years ago was out of sync with his advancing career and executive lifestyle.

1 John 5:21
_____

Little children, keep yourselves from idols.

God's Word

He opened the Bible his grandmother had given him for his confirmation, closed his eyes, and rummaged around with his index finger until it felt right to stop. Then he read the passage where his finger had settled. He should have known this was not a spiritually helpful practice when, after reading the chosen passage, he repeated the process until he finally found one that applied to him.

Hebrews 4:12

Indeed, the word of God is living and active, sharper than any two-edged sword, piercing until it divides soul from spirit, joints from marrow; it is able to judge the thoughts and intentions of the heart.

FRIENDSHIP

He prided himself on his ability to adapt to the changing moods and vagaries of strangers. Casual acquaintances considered him a remarkably kind and patient man, but his closest friends often felt used and abused by him. With those he knew best, he would make no adaptations, reserve no judgments, for his energy was spent being kind to those he would meet by chance.

HEBREWS 5:2-3

> He is able to deal gently with the ignorant and wayward, since he himself is subject to weakness; and because of this he my offer sacrifice for his own sins as well as for those of the people.

SINCERITY

His older brother once told him he had more charm than brains. He had replied, "Whatever works."

In the seventh grade, his teacher made him look up the word "sincere" and read the definition aloud. Then she told him to close the book and give the definition in his own words. He couldn't do it.

When he was twenty-one, after a few bottles of beer, he leaned over to the young woman next to him at the bar and whispered, "I truly love my girlfriend, but. . . ."

As he walked home from the woman's house later that night, he decided that for him, "Being sincere is getting what you want."

MATTHEW 12:33

"Either make the tree good, and its fruit good; or make the tree bad, and its fruit bad; for the tree is known by its fruit."

His Daughter's Daughter

Her mother gave her up for adoption when she was two days old. Her adoptive parents were always sure she belonged to them, but her grandfather refused to introduce her as his granddaughter. "She is not blood," he would say.

"Dad, I never thought you were a bigot," his daughter would scream at him.

"She may be your daughter," he would say, "and I'm glad you were generous enough to take her in and all—but she's not really my granddaughter."

At his funeral, two flower bouquets rested in the casket with him. One labeled "Grandchildren," and another labeled, "Daughter's Daughter." The grandchild he refused to acknowledge had paid for it herself.

She was also the only grandchild to show up at his funeral.

Mark 10:14

> But when Jesus saw this, he was indignant and said to them, "Let the little children come to me; do not stop them; for it is to such as these that the kingdom of God belongs."

THE CURE

When the boy was little and made too much noise, his drunken father would dangle him by his feet above the gas jet. "That quieted him down," the father would laugh, "put him right to sleep."

Later, in a treatment center, the father quit drinking. It was not because of the treatment, however, but because a nun gave him a holy card with a remnant of some saint's underwear. The father swears it was a miracle. "Alcoholics Anonymous," he said, "is for strong people; God is the only help of the weak."

The son never recovered. He walked and talked but his mind was gone. He wandered from one minimum wage job to another and drank. On a night he never remembered, he found a bed with a man who was HIV positive.

Later, as the father tucked the holy card into the shirt pocket on his son's corpse, he said, "The strong don't need miracles or God, only the weak and those who had no chance from the beginning."

MATTHEW 5:11

"Blessed are you when people revile you and persecute you and utter all kinds of evil against you falsely. . . . Rejoice and be glad, for your reward is great in heaven."

THE GOOD DEED

On a late fall day, after he had raked the leaves in his yard, he went to the hardware store and rented a machine that punched little holes in his lawn to break it up, give it some air, and help it grow better in the spring. Since he had rented the machine for the morning and his lawn was small, he decided to do the same for his neighbor's lawn.

"Do you have any idea what that's gonna do to my lawn?" his neighbor demanded after the deed was done.

"It's going to make your lawn grow better. I was just trying to be neighborly," the man said defensively.

"Well, now I'm going to have to mow it more often. I have enough to do already. Next time, keep your good deeds to yourself."

LUKE 10:27

> "You shall love the Lord your God with all your heart, and with all your soul, and with all your strength, and with all your mind; and your neighbor as yourself."

THE FACE OF THINGS

"The face of things!" That, she thought, was the rub. How could she tell what people were really thinking, what their motives were for being nice to her? A little voice inside her always said, "Be careful. You don't know what they really want, why they are doing this for you." It was that little voice that kept people at arms' length—and made sure she would always live alone.

1 SAMUEL 24:9

David said to Saul, "Why do you listen to the words of those who say, 'David seeks to do you harm'?"

First the Bad News

They couldn't believe it when their church burned to the ground, the work of an arsonist with a beef against God. The pastor called them together in a kind of huddle next to the charred remains.

"The bad news," he said, "is that we have no insurance against this sort of thing. The good news is that it's never money that brings us through our troubles, it's always God."

Luke 11:10

"For everyone who asks receives, and everyone who searches finds, and for everyone who knocks, the door will be opened."

AN UNEASY FIT

He is the newly named pastor of a large urban parish. The people there have a strong sense of identity and tradition. They do not know him as did those students and faculty where he taught for so many years. They eye him suspiciously, first impressions weighing in heavily. He is nervous, not sleeping well. He still smiles but his smiles are more rehearsed, less spontaneous. His jokes seem tight and thin.

Right now it is an uneasy fit. The people are afraid of him—afraid he will change them. He is afraid of the same thing—afraid they will change him. And their fears will come true.

That is grace.

ROMANS 8:28

We know that all things work together for good for those who love God, who are called according to his purpose.

UNDER CONTROL

Although her laugh is loud, it is never free. In fact, what you notice about her if you watch her long enough is that everything she shows the world is under control. It is the same way in her prayer, which is conscientious and direct but just short of free-flowing and spontaneous.

God will wait until they are face to face to tell her there is nothing he doesn't know about her and nothing so foolish as her pretense that there is nothing foolhardy in her.

1 CORINTHIANS 4:10

We are fools for the sake of Christ.

THE NEW CHURCH

When the parish decided they needed a new church, the council had grand schemes. "It is fitting," said the president of the parish council, "that we build a beautiful building for God."

The pastor, who would live with these people until he died, said, "Let's call a spade a spade. A church is not God's house; it's the house of God's people. God doesn't need a grand place to live. God has the heavens for a roof and the earth for a floor. If we are going to build a church, let's be honest enough to admit it is for ourselves. While it should be a worthy place where we give God honor and glory, no building can substitute for what belongs in our hearts."

2 SAMUEL 7:4-6

The word of the LORD came to Nathan: "Go and tell my servant David: Thus says the LORD: Are you the one to build me a house to live in? I have not lived in a house since the day I brought up the people of Israel from Egypt to this day, but I have been moving about in a tent and a tabernacle."

Paul

When they brought him to this country, he was a little butterball, an odd contrast to their slight builds. They'd never seen such a determined child. He refused to hold their hands as they walked from the plane to the parking lot. It took every bit of their combined energy just to keep up with him. His new American parents viewed him as a loving challenge from God.

They dubbed him Paul, a name with a history that should warn the rest of the world he was on the loose—and a reminder to him, should he need it, that conversion is always possible.

Acts 9:3-4

Now as he was going along and approaching Damascus, suddenly a light from heaven flashed around him. He fell to the ground and heard a voice saying to him, "Saul, Saul, why do you persecute me?"

Unburdened

She never held it against him that he had deserted her. They had known each other for six months when she told him a baby was on the way. He suggested an abortion, but she refused to kill the child within her. He fled, leaving her a note that said: "If you're smart, you'll get rid of this baby."

She kept the note, a reminder that it's not always easy to get rid of our problems—or the problem people in our lives.

Romans 4:7-8

"Blessed are those whose iniquities
     are forgiven,
   and whose sins are covered;
blessed is the one against whom
     the Lord will not reckon sin."

The Break-In

Every Saturday night the old man would walk into town for a few drinks at the local bar. He sat low on the bar stool, hunched forward over his beer. When someone talked to him he didn't raise his head but rather rolled his eyes up or to the side. He looked a hundred and may have been.

One Saturday, he announced that he was selling his land. The next week a young man showed up at his shack and offered him seven hundred dollars cash. The deal was settled. He moved into a boarding house in town, taking only an extra pair of overalls with him. He died that March.

Two days after he moved out some young boys broke into his shack and demolished everything— old crockery, furniture, and a mattress that they tore to shreds looking for the old man's secrets. They toppled his outhouse, broke the pump, and left with stories about the old man they couldn't tell without incriminating themselves in the break-in.

The young man who bought the land and shack went through the rubble and found two Indian head pennies from 1868. He found nothing else worth keeping.

Luke 12:2

"Nothing is covered up that will not be uncovered, and nothing secret that will not become known."

THE SOWER

She was the kind of woman who didn't shove wisdom down your throat, but let you absorb it without knowing it. It wasn't until you had moved away or almost forgotten her name that something she said, something she pointed to or alluded to, came back and showed you something you thought you'd never see or understand.

MARK 4:26-27

"The kingdom of God is as if someone would scatter seed on the ground, and would sleep and rise night and day, and the seed would sprout and grow, he does not know how."

THE TEACHER

As children they hated ice fishing with their father. It was always so cold out on the lake. Their father would not tolerate luxuries like fishing shanties or even stools to sit on. No, you simply stood and bore the cold and the boredom. Complaining was a sign of weakness, shivering a form of pouting, allowing the hole to freeze over a manifestation of laziness that would catch up with you later in life. The sons wanted to tell their father that this was not making them men so much as teaching them to fear being like him.

For his part, the father simply assumed that eventually his sons would enjoy the raw solitude and learn the secret that out here you could see God in the breath that froze on your mustache.

MARK 4:38

> And they woke him up and said to him, "Teacher, do you not care that we are perishing?"

THE UNTAMED HEART

She objected when he said, "You tame all the people in your life. Once you're through with them, they're not the same."

"That sounds manipulative," she said, "manipulative and deceitful."

"Oh no," he said, "You're quite open about what is acceptable and unacceptable behavior in your eyes. There's nothing underhanded about it, which shows just how powerful and practiced you've become."

That night she asked the God who had not yet tamed her heart to help her to let go.

MARK 5:4

The chains he wrenched apart,
and the shackles he broke in
pieces; and no one had the
strength to subdue him.

Mercy

Is it suspicion or hope that God will deal more mercifully with us than even our closest friends?

2 Samuel 24:14

David said to Gad, "I am in great distress; let us fall into the hand of the LORD, for his mercy is great; but let me not fall into human hands."

SAINTS IN EXILE?

She sat in the modern church, not quite sure where to look. The tabernacle was off in some side room. She could see no statues, and hanging where the cross belonged was a stainless steel sculpture that looked like something in the new shopping mall.

She worried about her children, but not because this church didn't look like a church. She was sure there were good people here. She worried because the children didn't know the saints, those spiritual giants who acted out of faith and did great things.

Where would her children learn they could suffer great things and still believe in God's love?

HEBREWS 11:32-34

And what more should I say? For time would fail me to tell of Gideon, Barak, Samson, Jephthah, of David and Samuel and the prophets–who through faith conquered kingdoms, administered justice, obtained promises, shut the mouths of lions, quenched raging fire, escaped the edge of the sword, won strength out of weakness, became mighty in war, put foreign armies to flight.

A Cloud of Witnesses

His father went back to the old country to find a wife. When he found one, she was half his age and promised to someone else. He took her in the middle of the night, promising she would see a land flowing with milk and honey.

During the Great Depression, they somehow managed to save enough money to buy a general store. Two days after they put up a sign proclaiming they were the new proprietors, the store burned to the ground. They had no insurance. His father never found regular work again, but the old man kept the dream alive: some day things will be better! He died the year his youngest son left home to pursue a career in art.

Like the father, the son helps create for others a world filled with possibilities and dreams waiting to come true. He fashions these dreams in bronze and wood and marble.

People cannot resist touching a dream. It is smooth and calming and it makes you forget your troubles.

HEBREWS 12:1

> Therefore, since we are surrounded by so great a cloud of witnesses, let us also lay aside every weight and the sin that clings so closely, and let us run with perseverance the race that is set before us.

Reach Out

He waited all afternoon, watching the other kids play football in the vacant lot next door. Why didn't they ask him to play? Late in the afternoon, it began to rain. They knocked at his door—not for him but to ask his mother if they could "toss the football around" in their basement, the largest in the neighborhood.

After thirty years of resenting that Saturday afternoon, the boy realized that if he had wanted to play football that much he should have just gone outside and played.

Hebrews 12:12-13

Therefore lift your drooping hands
and strengthen your weak knees, and
make straight paths for your feet, so
that what is lame may not be put out
of joint, but rather be healed.

READINESS

Every night before she goes to sleep, she puts out clean clothes to wear the next day—or for others to put on her for her eventual and inevitable trip to the mortuary.

PSALM 3:5

I lie down and sleep;
I wake again, for the LORD sustains me.

THE GOOD LIFE

He has to remind himself now and then that his life has been good; even the occasional sacrifices he perceived as great were not all that difficult.

HEBREWS 12:4

In your fight against sin you have not yet resisted to the point of shedding your blood.

Prayer Reflections

Praying when you don't believe in a God who listens is like talking to yourself in the mirror. It's amazing how much the person in the mirror looks like you and wants only what you want.

Psalm 86:5-6

For you, O Lord, are good and forgiving,
abounding in steadfast love to all
who call on you.
Give ear, O Lord, to my prayer;
listen to my cry of supplication.

PEACE

This morning she came to Mass because her
father is dying. The man she once thought invincible, the man who made her earn her determination, is passing on. She no longer recognizes him.
He is already crossing into pure light.

The priest has been ordained only a few months.
He is awkward in his vestments and holds his
arms straight out from his sides like a little boy
who still thinks he can fly. He has a picture in his
head of what his face is supposed to look like
when he's praying and he arranges his expres-
sions appropriately. He modulates his voice to a
level of sincerity unsubstantiated by experience.

At the sign of peace he seeks her out. He sees her
distress but does not understand it. "Peace," he
says kindly.

She hesitates, looks at him, and says quietly,
"Yes. May we all rest in peace."

HEBREWS 12:14

Pursue peace with everyone,
and the holiness without which
no one will see the Lord.

KEEP MOVING

She married late in life to a widower who had owned his own business and been a mayor of their small town. Shortly after the wedding, she sold her house and completely redecorated his. She wiped out all signs of his previous life, favoring shades of pink from foyer to bathroom to living room. They also purchased matching Cadillacs.

Now they are both old and ailing. He has cancer and she a blood disease. Although it's hard for them to get around, they still love traveling. On a trip to Branson, Missouri she was so sick from her medication she had to take along a vomit tray.

Before they left, a good friend suggested they stay home until she was better. She explained to her friend, "If my husband and I stop moving, we will die, and I don't want either of us to die."

PROVERBS 9:10-11

> The fear of the LORD is the beginning
>   of wisdom,
>   and the knowledge of the Holy One
>   is insight.
> For by me your days will be multiplied,
>   and years will be added to your life.

COMPASSION

God doesn't have as hard a time remembering we are creatures who need care as we have remembering we are creatures who need God.

PSALM 103:13-14

As a father has compassion for his
    children,
    so the Lord has compassion for those
    who fear him
For he knows how we were made;
    he remembers that we are dust.

To Be a Man

It was the first time his children had seen him frightened, crying, unsure of himself. His oldest son, just at the age where he was trying to figure out what it meant to be a man, tried not to show how upset he was.

"Dad," he asked finally, "what do you do when things are this bad?"

"Pray," was all his father said.

PSALM 32:6

Therefore, let all who are faithful
   offer prayer to you;
at a time of distress, the rush of mighty
   waters
   shall not reach them.

Growing Up

He has been driving this section of highway since he was eighteen—a two-hour drive from where he lives to where his parents live. No matter how often he does it, the same memories come back to him as he drives along—his mother's cooking, his father's favorite chair, the smooth floors of their well-kept house, the mismatched tools in his father's garage, the crucifix hanging in his parents' bedroom.

These memories anchor his feelings that he has indeed grown up and needs to be about his own life.

Luke 2:51-52

Then he went down with them and came to Nazareth, and was obedient to them. His mother treasured all these things in her heart. And Jesus increased in wisdom and in years, and in divine and human favor.

GOODNESS REMEMBERED

There are only a few of them left now at the Motherhouse. They have never been a large order of sisters, but they had banded together against all odds at the turn of the century and worked hard to teach poor immigrants. Now each year fewer and fewer of them gather in the mornings and evenings to pray. Yet even in their sure demise they recall how good God has been to them.

PSALM 48:9

We ponder your steadfast love, O God,
in the midst of your temple.

HOSPITALITY

Of all the things she has changed in her home—couches and appliances that came and went, curtains that were replaced with blinds, floor tiles that have been replaced three times—the one thing that has never changed is the sign she tacked up in the entryway the day they moved in forty-two years ago.

It reads simply: "Welcome to this house. May all who enter here be blessed, for they bring a blessing."

HEBREWS 13:2

Do not neglect to show hospitality to strangers, for by doing that some have entertained angels without knowing it.

THE ODDBALL

Had things turned out differently, he would be retired now and tending raspberries in the mid-summer sun. Perhaps he would have worn a straw hat, the kind his grandfather used to wear; perhaps he would have taught his grandchildren how to tend the canes in the fall, cutting out the old worn ones to make room for younger bushes. In winter he would have sat at his kitchen table in the early morning and had homemade jam—the fruit of his labor—on his toast.

As it is, most people simply look at him and walk away, shaking their heads sadly or commenting about how you see more and more oddballs on the street every day.

ISAIAH 53:3
___

> He was despised and rejected by others;
>   a man of suffering and acquainted
>   with infirmity;
> and as one from whom others hide their
>   faces;
>   he was despised, and we held him of
>   no account.

MARRIAGE

She strode out of the bar with all the assurance a little booze and a lot of laughs can give. She had crinkly blond hair—either from peroxide or hair spray. It was poofy and wavy and swirled around her face like cotton candy. She wore a black and white polka-dot pants suit, tight-fitted against her body, jarring in the bright sun. She was an icon of bad taste.

Everyone was her friend that day. She waved at old ladies and gentlemen with canes, delivery people and postal workers. She was halfway down the street before her husband came out of the bar and caught up with her.

When they got to the car, she waited for him to unlock and open the door for her. He reached over and ran his hands through her hair, crumpling it into tight little balls here and there all over her head. She grabbed his hand firmly and, in a moment of mutual joy, held it to her lips.

HEBREWS 13:4

Let marriage be held in honor by all.

HARD REALITIES

He was born scrawny, all legs and arms. When his sisters and brothers held him, his elbows and knees dug into their armpits and stomachs, making him hard to hold for any length of time, so they stopped holding him. Too soon and too young he learned to fend for himself.

Things didn't change much when he got older. He grew up pretty much a loner—not shy or introverted, but thoughtful and reserved. He married the only woman he ever dated, one who enjoyed the angles of his body from their first tentative moments of affection.

She did her best to fatten him up, but eventually was content to love him just as he was. They raised three children, two girls and a boy, who— like their mother—were soft and eagerly forgiving of the hard way he felt when he held them.

Six months after his wife died, his older daughter found him sitting at the kitchen table looking at an old goldfish bowl filled with grocery receipts. When she asked what he was doing, he answered, "Trying to figure out how much it costs to keep me alive." Then, reaching around him with both her arms, she held him against the hard realities of growing old alone.

HEBREWS 13:5

> Be content with what you have,
> for he has said, "I will never leave
> you or forsake you."

GRANDMOTHER'S ROSARY

When he watched his grandmother holding her beads and saying Hail Marys so quickly she slurred the words together, he shook his head. He was sure he would never pray like her. He was too young to understand that her faith was much stronger than the plastic beads she fingered so rapidly.

HEBREWS 13:7

Remember your leaders, those who
spoke the word of God to you;
consider the outcome of their way of
life, and imitate their faith.

REPUTATION

Knowing a person's reputation—even that of Jesus—isn't enough to make you change the way you live.

MARK 6:14

King Herod heard of it, for
Jesus' name had become known.

SNOWFLAKES

On a cold February morning, he looked out his
kitchen window. It was still dark, although the
shadows cast by the street lights told him it had
snowed again. It would take him an hour to shovel
it. He pulled out a saucepan, drew some water
from the tap, put it on to boil, and placed a tea bag
in a cup. He wanted something warm before he
went outside.

He went to the stove and poured the boiling water
into his cup. As he stood there dunking the tea
bag, he watched the wind pick up the snow and
sweep it into drifts. He contemplated how many
snowflakes it took to create a decent-size drift and
wondered if you could do an experiment to count
them as they mounted up. He supposed it could
be done by weight, if you knew how much a
snowflake weighed . . . and if they all weighed the
same.

It was just another problem he would never solve.

SIRACH 1:1-2

All wisdom is from the Lord,
  and with him it remains forever.
The sand of the sea, the drops of rain,
  and the days of eternity–who can
    count them?
The height of heaven, the breadth of
  the earth,
  the abyss, and wisdom–who can
    search them out?

Morning Mass

On cold days, she always walked to morning Mass, preferring to save the wear and tear on her old car.

The exercise was good for her. And she always felt so holy when she got there.

Sirach 1:11
_____

The fear of the Lord is glory and
exultation,
and gladness and a crown of
rejoicing.

Coma

The two of them sat by the side of their eight-year-old son's bed. Yesterday he was chasing balls in their yard; today he is in a coma. Their friends don't know what to say to them, and they don't know what to say to their friends. The couple tried praying, but they received no comfort.

"Perhaps," they thought, "if we had prayed more before, we would have something to say now."

JOEL 2:13

Return to the LORD, your God,
    for he is gracious and merciful,
slow to anger, and abounding in
    steadfast love.

THE BETTER PURPOSE

They were married four years before their son was born. They were not easy years. Both of them were strong-willed, uncompromising, and easily hurt.

They used up the old roles quickly. She wasn't a good cook. He worked long hours and came home crabby and demanding. She didn't know how to manage the household money. He didn't make enough. She got silly on a little wine. He drank too much.

When their son was born they discovered a new resolve and a better purpose.

<hr>

DEUTERONOMY 30:19-20

> I have set before you life and death,
> blessings and curses. Choose life so
> that you and your descendants may
> live, loving the LORD your God,
> obeying him, and holding fast to him.

THE SECOND WIFE

He promised his first wife on her deathbed that he wouldn't remarry until their two daughters could fend for themselves. He kept his word. His daughters were seventeen and nineteen when he married again. His new wife had no time for his daughters, and they left home as soon as they could.

When he died, his daughters mourned him, but they never visited the second wife.

HEBREWS 12:15

See to it that no one fails to obtain the grace of God; that no root of bitterness springs up and causes trouble.

THE STRAWBERRY PATCH

Long before the last of the snow was off the fields, she would walk out to the strawberry patch. Shading her eyes against the glare of the late winter sun, she would look for exposed bits of straw and heart-shaped dried leaves, proof that the plants were still where she left them. Was the winter too hard, the frost too deep? Would there be strawberries this year?

In June, hunched over with the sun warming her back, her broad-brimmed straw hat hiding the delight in her eyes, she ate as many strawberries as she put into her basket.

How could she have doubted there would be strawberries this year?

ISAIAH 58:11

The LORD will guide you continually,
and satisfy your needs in parched
places,
and make your bones strong;
and you shall be like a watered garden,
like a spring of water,
whose waters never fail.

Baking Bread

Her mother died when she was two. She lived with her father, grandfather, and younger sister. She was cooking for all of them by the time she was nine. It was not good cooking, but serviceable. It filled their bellies and made them round reflections of each other.

Her father loved the gravy from fried meats, especially pork. He would say, "Now if only we had some of your mother's fresh baked bread to soak up this gravy, wouldn't that be great? Wouldn't that be just like Christmas in July?"

She tried to bake bread, but her rolls came out like buffalo chips and her loaves of sweet dough like putty.

There was no one to teach her, no one to tell her that baking good bread was not a science but an act of love.

Exodus 16:4

Then the Lord said to Moses, "I am going to rain bread from heaven for you, and each day the people shall go out and gather enough for that day."

The Parish Council

Everyone knew he had moved into the rectory with the priest and the priest's two maiden sisters. He was a carpenter by trade and fairly pious. He went to daily Mass, sitting several pews behind the two sisters.

There were rumors about him. Some said he had taken up with one of the priest's sisters, but no one knew which one. Neither doted on him publicly, and he appeared to show no favorites. This only increased the speculation.

The parish council called a special session. They wanted to know who he was and what he was doing there. At least that was what they said. What they really wanted to know, prurient interest aside, was whether his rent money was going to the priest or to the parish.

The pastor produced a check written out to the parish for one year's rent. It was a short meeting.

LEVITICUS **19:1**

> The LORD spoke to Moses, saying:
> Speak to all the congregation of
> the people of Israel and say to
> them: You shall be holy, for I, the
> LORD, your God, am holy.

THE ROLLER COASTER

He teasingly called her Tonto, for she was his ever-faithful companion. Ever since they were children, she had always been there for him. Each time another relationship of his bit the dust, he would call her for sympathy and consolation.

Of course, he never knew how she felt about him. She would have cut off her tongue rather than tell him. So she'd just climb back on that roller coaster to ride the highs and the lows, bracing herself for the inevitable sudden stops.

ROMANS 13:8

Owe no one anything, except to love one another; for the one who loves another has fulfilled the law.

Tried and Failed

At forty-four, she was tired. She had become an advocate for the residents in the nursing home because she believed she could make lives better.

She told her best friend, "My colleagues keep undoing everything I try. They say either it can't be done or it's impossible to do or it's already been done and has failed."

Romans 14:4

Who are you to pass judgment on servants of another? It is before their own lord that they stand or fall. And they will be upheld, for the Lord is able to make them stand.

STICK PEOPLE

She can't print yet—except her first name—so she draws pictures of what she sees in church: stick people with uniformly roundish faces, eyes agog, occasionally with one arm or leg too many. She has only two choices for hair color, bright yellow like her own or brown like her father's. The stick man with his hands outstretched, no hair, and an indistinct green blob covering most of his torso is the priest.

She hands the pictures to the priest at the end of Mass. He smiles. He doesn't consider the pictures but the years her parents waited for her, how God knew her name before they did. He sees how she melts the sternest face her father can muster when she's being particularly strong-willed. He notes how God has taken the blue from the sky and put it in her eyes.

For just a moment, he sees her the way he hopes God will see him when they meet face to face.

PSALM 138:8

The LORD will fulfill his
purpose for me.

Free-Falling

Yesterday his wife said she wanted a divorce. It was nothing new. She has repeated this threat often, along with a litany of his faults: he's too weak or too dull; he eats with his mouth open; he doesn't pay any attention to her; he has grown old and fat; he is a poor provider.

He listened as always and then called her doctor. "She's off her medication again. I'll try to bring her in."

She fought him all the way to the clinic. When she went into the consulting room, he took a seat in the waiting room and picked up a magazine. He saw an ad with a skydiver holding a can of beer. He thought to himself, "You can't drink beer when you're free-falling."

Then he put down the magazine and walked out of the clinic.

Ezekiel 18:25

> Yet you say, "The way of the Lord is unfair!" Hear now, O house of Israel: Is my way unfair? Is it not your ways that are unfair?

THE VOW

On the day she had walked out the convent door, she vowed that she would never enter a church again.

She was good at keeping that promise.

SIRACH 17:29

How great is the mercy of the Lord,
And his forgiveness for those
who return to him!

OLD FRIENDS

He was driving to meet a priest friend who had just moved into a new rectory. It was in a small town, on a ridge above green valleys. He was looking forward to dinner and some friendly conversation. They had been friends since childhood and counted on certain things from each other, though they met only once a year.

He pulled into the driveway and entered the kitchen through a side door. Heading straight for the refrigerator, he pulled out a beer (politeness between them was predicated on their abiding affection for each other, not protocol).

He went into the dining room and found two strangers sitting down to supper. "Where's John?" he asked. They stared blankly at him and told him to have a seat. In a few moments, the door bell rang and John walked in. The rectory was on the other side of the street.

He went with his friend to the rectory. They sat on the porch, reminisced about the old days, and worried about the future—as aging men do.

MATTHEW 17:1

> Jesus took with him Peter and James and his brother John and led them up on a high mountain, by themselves.

THE HOLES BETWEEN US

He's always had too much hair and now it is silver gray—a kind of wild grace that balances his even temper and belies his passion for God. His bearing and build deny his fifty years. His shoulders form a perfect perpendicular to his spine, which he pulls straight up. It's not pride that makes him stand so straight but a sense of the importance of every moment and every person he encounters.

The row of chairs beside him in the funeral parlor was vacant. A woman entered, chose a seat at the opposite end of the row, and buried her face in her hands. Without hesitating, he went over to her, offered his hand, and sat next to her. It was a brief gesture of genuine human warmth and grace between strangers.

Then he turned to her and said, "You know, I think it's the holes between us that cause us the most pain."

PSALM 79:8

Let your compassion come
    speedily to meet us,
for we are brought very low.

THE SACRIFICE

Long before Lent began, they struck a bargain. He would give up sweets and she would give up alcohol. The first week they did well, each denying the peculiar urge that makes what we give up so much more desirable.

On Tuesday of the second week of Lent, she sent him e-mail at work: "It's been a bad day here. I've turned mean." He sent back a snappy reply: "You think it's been bad for you. My co-workers are hiding from me."

She responded: "Tonight I shall feast on fudge and chocolate cake for you. You shall drink a bottle of wine for me. And together at table, we shall pray for forgiveness of our sins."

PSALM 60:1

> O God, you have rejected us, broken
>   our defenses;
>   you have been angry;
>   Now restore us!

Jump Start

On snowy winter mornings he would stop on his way to the university to push people out of the snow. He helped old ladies across the street. This morning he strung cables to a roommate's battery and jumped his car.

Later, when it was time for him to leave, his own car wouldn't start; the battery was dead.

JEREMIAH 18:20

Is evil a recompense for good?

REDEMPTION

Although the church was empty, she spoke softly to the priest. "I want to know what sin is."

The priest replied, "Sin is a break in our relationship with God, with other people, or even with ourselves."

"How many sins need to pile up before I must confess them?" she asked.

"Oh, about a hundred," the priest said.

"Why a hundred?" she asked.

"Because it's a good round number, and most sins are not that heavy. After all, Jesus carried all of them on his back."

"You're joking with me," she said, finally smiling and speaking in a normal tone.

"Maybe," said the priest, "but we need to keep sin in perspective. Redemption is always more important than sin."

PSALM 25:7

> Do not remember the sins of my youth
> or my transgressions;
> according to your steadfast love
> remember me,
> for your goodness' sake, O Lord!

THE DREAM SLAYER

At forty-four, she was in the full swing of her mid-life crisis. "I want to do something valuable with my life," she told a friend.

It wasn't that her life had been unproductive. She had raised two children, worked admirably at a job in a social service agency, was well thought of by the people who knew her. She just felt dull and pointless. With resolve she told her friend, "I'm going to adopt an abandoned child."

Three weeks later, the friend asked about her adoption plans.

"I can't sleep at night," she responded. "I keep having the nightmare that I am holding a baby. I stumble and fall and drop the baby."

Her friend made light of her fears: "Maybe you should start by helping at the humane society. Cats always seem to land on their feet."

GENESIS 37:19-20

Here comes this dreamer. Come now, let us kill him and throw him into one of the pits; then we shall say that a wild animal has devoured him, and we shall see what will become of his dreams.

Marvelous Things

She grew up in her aunt and uncle's home, abandoned by her parents and forgotten by her siblings. The man she was marrying owned a scrap metal business. He had a big crane to move the metal around the yard and load it onto the big trucks that hauled it away. His fingernails were stained black and his hands were rough, but he loved her. He purchased a new mobile home and put it on a hill overlooking the scrap yard.

When they came home from their honeymoon, he carried her across the threshold of their new home, led her to the window over the kitchen sink, and pointed to the crane.

There, at the very top, were two large gold rings intertwined.

Micah 7:15

> As in the days when you came out of
> the land of Egypt,
> show us marvelous things.

THE FLAME

The deacon has an uncanny knack of attracting odd people. They are drawn to him as moths to a flame—soul mates who attach themselves to him while he's minding his own business.

A complete stranger standing next to him in line at a convenience store said to him one day: "You're too skinny." Most people would have ignored the comment, but he invited the man to have coffee with him. The man began to comment on his miserable, lonely life: "I'm an alcoholic. I don't drink anymore, but I'm an alcoholic."

"How did you stop drinking?" the deacon asked.

"I hit rock bottom. The other alcoholics even threw me out of Alcoholics Anonymous. They said I gave alcoholics a bad name. Can you believe it?"

That rude stranger, a designer of greeting cards, now sends the deacon a Christmas card every month throughout the year.

JOHN 4:6-7, 9

Jesus, tired out by his journey, was sitting by the well. It was about noon. A Samaritan woman came to draw water, and Jesus said to her, "Give me a drink." . . . The Samaritan woman said to him, "How is it that you, a Jew, ask a drink of me, a woman of Samaria?"

THE BLESSING

She wanted the priest to give her a blessing. "When I was a little girl in a Catholic school," she said, "every time I saw the pastor, he would put his hand on my head and give me a blessing. Things seemed to go better with that blessing sitting on my head."

The priest said, "I'll give you a blessing, but it's not magic. You are already blessed."

She had never looked at it that way before.

1 CORINTHIANS 1:4-5

> I give thanks to my God always for you because of the grace of God that has been given you in Christ Jesus, for in every way you have been enriched in him.

Ever Ready

He was always looking down the road, thinking ahead, making and remaking plans. He didn't want to be caught off guard. He liked to have all his bases covered.

He got things done way ahead of time. This did not endear him to the people with whom he worked or with his family. His children laughed at him when he sorted out the Christmas decorations as he took down the tree so they would be in the correct order next year. They got annoyed when he wanted to leave early for practices and recitals. They disliked going to church with him because they were always the first ones there and had to be silent for such a long time.

Driving to work one cold morning, he hit a patch of ice and slammed into a telephone pole. His will was up to date, his insurance paid ahead. His funeral instructions were complete and neatly typed.

Luke 12:40

"You also must be ready, for the Son of Man is coming at an unexpected hour."

Her Own Private Cross

Her children don't go to church anymore. It is her own private cross to bear—she who had always gone, always believed, always been faithful.

In the beginning, when her husband objected to baptizing the children, she didn't argue or press the point. She baptized them herself, secretly—first her son, then five years later her daughter. When they were old enough, she would take them with her to early morning Mass while her husband was asleep.

She wondered why her faith never took in them.

DEUTERONOMY 4:9

> But take care and watch yourselves closely, so as neither to forget the things that your eyes have seen nor to let them slip from your mind all the days of your life; make them known to your children and your children's children.

In Memoriam

He rises early on Memorial Day. He is old enough now where that doesn't bother him. He doesn't sleep all the way through most nights anyway. Sleeping late was something he only thought he wanted to do when he couldn't because he had to get up for work.

He puts on dress pants and a white shirt. He finds his old army hat with its campaign pins on it. He leaves for the cemetery where he meets other men his age, boyhood friends who went to war with him.

It is cold. There are not many bystanders to watch and listen as they make speeches to the graves with flags on them. No one cries and no one tries to sing the national anthem. They shoot a few rifles, not in bold unison but in a rat-a-tat sequence which brings smiles to some faces, and—in more ways than anyone wants to admit—critiques the glory of war. Then they go down to the VFW hall and have a few beers. More people show up for the beer than for the ceremony.

Isaiah 60:2

For darkness shall cover the earth,
    and thick darkness the peoples;
but the LORD will arise upon you,
    and his glory will appear over you.

Choices

She had spent most of her life making wrong choices. This time she was determined it would be different. It was the second marriage for both of them. She had stuck it out, not because of love or passion but because she was too afraid of the pain of another divorce.

Now, as he lay collapsed on their living room floor, she dialed 911, knowing that if she did it slowly enough he would be dead before help arrived.

Wisdom 1:6

For wisdom is a kindly spirit,
but will not free blasphemers from the
     guilt of their words;
because God is witness of their inmost
     feelings.

THE PARABLE

Sitting in the religious studies class, he felt stupid. "Of course you know this story from your Sunday school classes," said the professor.

No. He didn't know this story.

He tried to remember those Wednesday evenings he sat with his friends looking sullen and forbidding to the well-meaning volunteers who tried to teach them religion. What had he learned? What had he listened to? He couldn't remember anything.

As much as he wanted to believe, he suddenly realized that he didn't know what to believe in.

LUKE 8:11-12

"Now the parable is this: The seed is the word of God. The ones on the path are those who have heard; then the devil comes and takes away the word from their hearts, so that they may not believe and be saved."

BLINDNESS

They were flying home to Kansas City. Her father had died. They had borrowed the money for their air fare from the man for whom they both worked. Their daughter alternated sitting on their laps, a free fare. She was quiet and watched the other passengers with the same sad eyes of her parents.

When lunch came, they begged an extra cup of ice cream from the flight attendant for their daughter, but she said there was only enough for the paying passengers. A passenger across the aisle reached over with his untouched ice cream. "Here take mine."

For just a moment, their eyes almost seemed to smile.

LUKE 9:47-48

> Jesus, aware of their inner thoughts, took a little child and put it by his side, and said to them, "Whoever welcomes this child in my name welcomes me, and whoever welcomes me welcomes the one who sent me; for the least among all of you is the greatest."

The Carpenter

In the seminary, he was the fair-haired boy: bright, challenging, concerned about all the right things, fun-loving yet with a keen eye for ecclesiastical politics. He protected himself against his mistakes by courting the favor of professors who promised him a bright future. He knew how to make things happen—for himself and for others.

He did some good things. He led a student revolt when one professor refused to answer questions in class because questions were "too distracting." The professor was assigned to a parish the next year.

He also did some funny things. When the rector put up concrete barricades to keep students from parking too close to the lawn, he went to the army surplus store and bought helmets and green overcoats and had students march up and down in front of the barricades. The rector had the ramparts cut down to scale.

He was ordained and remained a priest for ten years. Then he left to become a carpenter.

PSALM 25:10

All the paths of the LORD are steadfast
     love and faithfulness,
     for those who keep his covenant and
     his decrees.

THE ROUND TABLE

She is the sort of person who makes you believe in stereotypes. Flowing, silver-gray hair, olive coloring, a thick accent, pudgy hands and strong fingers from kneading bread. Her eyes are kind beyond belief. She is the epitome of Italian grandmas.

Each March nineteenth, she opens her restaurant to anyone who wants to come to eat. It doesn't matter whether you are rich or poor, starving or overweight. If you stand in line long enough, you'll get a meal. Everyone gets to order off the menu. Her sons try to explain that she could find better, and cheaper, ways to help others. She will hear none of it.

"Life," she says, "is a round table. Whatever you put on it eventually comes back to you."

JAMES 2:15-16

> If a brother or sister is naked and
> lacks daily food, and one of you
> says to them, "Go in peace; keep
> warm and eat your fill," and yet
> you do not supply their bodily
> needs, what is the good of that?

Lost

She walked along the same sidewalk in the same part of town every Monday. On Tuesdays she went to a different part of town, on Wednesdays to still a different part, and so on through the week. That was her life—walking the streets but always the same streets. Then she would come home late afternoons and put up her feet on the old footstool in her one-room apartment and rest.

Isaiah 49:14-15

But Zion said, "The LORD has
    forsaken me;
    my Lord has forgotten me."
Can a woman forget her nursing
    child,
    or show no compassion for the
    child of her womb?
Even these may forget,
    yet I will not forget you.

THE GRAVEN IMAGE

When he was born, his great-uncle gave him a solid gold medal of St. George. "He's too young now to appreciate it," his great-uncle had told his parents, "but some day he'll live up to that saint. He'll do a lot of good in this world and beat down a lot of bad."

Twenty-one years later, with a thirst burning in his belly so hot his saliva has dried up, he walks into a pawn shop and asks the going rate for gold.

PSALM 106:19-20

They made a calf at Horeb
    and worshiped a cast image.
They exchanged the glory of God
    for the image of an ox that eats grass.

Righteousness

He always claimed his sister was mean and selfish. She had not, he boasted, inherited their mother's goodness—as he had.

On this day he calls his sister, who lives in Nevada. He reminds her that their mother is lonely and that she should call. She takes the rebuke politely, says nothing in return to suggest she is angry or hurt.

When he hangs up, he looks at the picture of his mother next to the phone. There is a man's arm around her, his father's arm.

He had cut his father out of the picture long ago.

Matthew 7:1-2

"Do not judge, so that you may not be judged. For with the judgment you make you will be judged, and the measure you give will be the measure you get."

Beauty

As a little girl, she had the prettiest face on the block. As a young woman, she wasn't just pretty, she was strikingly beautiful. She married a man who supplied the perfect frame for her good looks, handsome but not overly so, good features but with enough flaws to highlight how perfect she was. A few years later, their marriage fell apart and they separated.

One night at a party, the host's dog attacked her for no apparent reason. She was sitting on a couch when the dog lunged for her face. It took thirty-three stitches to close the gap, which ran from just below her eye to her jaw. Months later, after several surgeons had repaired her face, her friends noticed a change in her.

Some internal goodness had finally bled to the surface.

Romans 5:3-5

And not only that, but we also boast in our sufferings, knowing that suffering produces endurance, and endurance produces character, and character produces hope, and hope does not disappoint us, because God's love has been poured into our hearts through the Holy Spirit that has been given to us.

ALZHEIMER'S

Some people can list every wrong ever done to them, every hurt they have endured, every time they were left out in the dark by the people they thought were their friends. He was blessed with an unclear memory that could boast only shadows of people, vague recollections, large gaps.

In this way he was favored by God, for he had suffered much. As a child, he lay in a body cast for months while doctors stretched and straightened some curvature in his spine. When he was an adolescent, his peers rejected him, not in a passing way but in a lingering, dulling way that made those preteen years seem to last forever. When he was older and could find no woman who would promise to love him and him alone, he settled for one-night stands and lonely days. But he remembers very little of this today.

Today he is alive. The sun, which he supposed must have been out yesterday, is shining now and warm on his face. The people on the sidewalk in front of him are laughing.

And all he can see from where he stands is this moment.

ROMANS 6:11

You must consider yourselves dead to sin and alive to God in Christ Jesus.

FALSE TESTIMONY

The man sued the university for firing him. He claimed it was because he was old and they wanted to make room for a young man who had published a lot of research. In truth, the dean of the school of business had spent years trying to get him into a treatment center for his drinking.

When word of the lawsuit made the local paper, no one at the Retired Businessman's Association would speak to the dean anymore. This saddened him because he had always enjoyed their company and had attempted to organize them to mentor university students. At their spring meeting, they voted to suspend the mentoring program.

The dean remained silent. He never explained what had really happened.

SUSANNA 1:42-43

> Then Susanna cried out with a loud voice, and said, "O eternal God, you know what is secret and are aware of all things before they come to be; you know that these men have given false evidence against me. And now I am to die, though I have done none of the wicked things they have charged against me!"

THE ROOMER

Something went wrong when he was conceived, some genetic particle got lost in the rush to life. He had two personalities: one that people could live with, one that people could not.

He made his way from halfway house to halfway house. None would keep him long. Finally, with no place else to go, he rented a room from an old woman who reminded him of his mother. She spent hours accommodating him, giving in to his demands, trying to anticipate what would set him off, relieved when he returned to normal. As time went on, her gentleness seemed to win out over his afflictions. She became his first real friend.

One Friday in March, she slipped and broke her hip. He visited her every day in the hospital, bringing her spring flowers from her own garden. When she came home, he was there to take care of all her needs. And he knew at last why God had created him.

GALATIANS 6:1

My friends, if anyone is detected in a transgression, you who have received the Spirit should restore such a one in a spirit of gentleness.

UNPACKED BOXES

A third of her basement was filled with boxes she never fully unpacked. Occasionally she'd rummage through them to find an item she remembered having at the old house.

Somewhere in the boxes was her divorce decree, which she never needed because she never married again. She had promised, "You alone will I love," to the man who had run off with another woman.

And she had meant it.

REVELATION 2:10

"Be faithful until death, and I will give you the crown of life."

The Name Game

He has thickened with age and sports a full beard. He still wears tennis shoes and jeans, but they look odd on him now that he's nearing fifty.

When he was twenty-five, he had his name legally changed from Irvin to Roc. It fit him then. He was a musician. He still is a musician, but the name no longer works. His children always had problems when they had to fill out forms that asked for their father's name. "Roc can't possibly be your father's *real* name," their teachers would say.

"But that *is* his real name," they'd insist.

Sometimes we grow into our names . . . and sometimes we grow out of them.

1 CORINTHIANS 13:11

When I was a child, I spoke like a child, I thought like a child, I reasoned like a child; when I became an adult, I put an end to childish ways.

The Rock

Driving back from her parents' house one Sunday, she marveled at the large bluffs along the highway. Her face darkened as she noticed that someone had spray-painted something on one of the most prominent outcroppings. In large letters someone had written the words, "Jesus is Lord."

When she arrived at home, she said to her husband, "I was so angry when I saw what they had done to those beautiful bluffs. Jesus may be Lord, but you don't have to shout about it."

Psalm 18:1-2

> I love you, O Lord my strength.
> The Lord is my rock, my fortress,
> and my deliverer,
> my God, my rock in whom
> I take refuge,
> my shield, and the horn of my
> salvation, my stronghold.

THE BROTHER

At seventy-seven, he still looked impressive, especially with his miter and crosier. He had been a bishop for eighteen years before retiring. His replacement was half his age and had a long way to go to match his wisdom.

When he was sixteen and mowing the lawn for an orphanage, he became friends with an eight-year-old boy whom the rest of the kids didn't like. He went home and begged his parents to adopt the child nobody wanted.

At his ordination as bishop, his adopted brother proclaimed the first reading.

EZEKIEL 37:27-28

My dwelling shall be with them; and I will be their God, and they shall be my people. Then the nations shall know that I the LORD sanctify Israel, when my sanctuary is among them forevermore.

Ash Wednesday

He took his place in line with everyone else on Ash Wednesday. The pastor spoke the words gently: "Remember that you are dust and you will return to dust."

The man returned to the pew and hunched down on his knees. A week ago, his doctor had told him that everything inside him was shutting down. Bits of ash from the cross on his forehead fell into his eyes, causing tears to fall—tears he had been holding back all week.

John 16:22

> "So you have pain now; but I will see you again, and your hearts will rejoice, and no one will take your joy from you."

A Good Heart

His heart was always in the right place, even if he fumbled most of his attempts at doing good for others. When trying to convince someone to help move a needy family, he talked too much. When asking his neighbors for donations for worthy causes, he pushed too hard. When arguing before the City Council against ordinances that would adversely affect poorer neighborhoods, he wouldn't sit down.

People hated to see him coming.

Isaiah 42:2-3

He will not cry or lift up his voice,
    or make it heard in the street;
a bruised reed he will not break,
    and a dimly burning wick he will not
        quench;
he will faithfully bring forth justice.

God's Secret Agent

She picks over the vigil lights under the icon of Our Mother of Perpetual Help in the same way she chooses apples at the grocery store. She lets no one rush her.

She lights a candle each day and prays—not for her own troubles, which are clear and plentiful, but for the lost and forgotten causes, for the situations and the people no one else prays for.

She is God's secret agent, battling underground suffering on its own terms.

Isaiah 49:6

"I will give you as a light to the
   nations,
      that my salvation may reach to the
         end of the earth."

HUNGERS

Halfway home from work she remembers her husband asked her to pick up cereal for breakfast. She turns into the grocery store parking lot where she has spent Saturday mornings for the past twenty years. She knows where the cereal is but goes first to the deli to look for a quick supper. On a whim she buys four lamb chops and some mint jelly.

By the time her husband arrives home, dinner is ready. He asks if she remembered the cereal. She is startled. She forgot to buy it.

Then he smells the lamb and says, "How did you know I was thinking of my mother's roast lamb and mint jelly? My mouth has been watering for some all day."

ISAIAH 50:4

Morning by morning he wakens–
    wakens my ear
        to listen as those who are taught.

THE GOAL

When he was born, his parents named him Christ, not pronounced as in Jesus Christ but as in Christopher. At his baptism, his father said, "We chose this name not to remind him where he came from but where he is going. The people and places he will leave behind will survive without him. But if he forgets where he's going, it's doubtful he'll survive himself."

JOHN 13:2-4

And during supper Jesus, knowing that the Father had given all things into his hands, and that he had come from God and was going to God, got up from the table, took off his outer robe, and tied a towel around himself.

EVIL

The idea that human beings can be truly evil presupposes we have more power than we really have. When people perform evil acts, it is from greed or anger or envy or sickness—all weaknesses of the flesh. Evil, real evil, has a life of its own and knows no reasons. It comes and goes on the wind. It doesn't care who is struck down or what is ruined or how many people burn in unquenchable fire. Evil doesn't notice the parched land it leaves behind nor the saplings that are hacked off at the root.

ROMANS: 7:21

So I find it to be a law that when I want to do what is good, evil lies close at hand.

FIRST LOVES

She didn't agree with the speaker when he said, "Too often our memories only go back as far as our last hurt. Rarely do our memories go back to our first loves."

She had never been able to get her first love out of her head. He was tall and thin, with thick black hair that rose like a surfer's wave on the top of his head. When he looked at her, the color of her world changed. Even though she hadn't seen him for thirty years, she was still trying to make herself into someone he would desire.

As she walked, she noticed that someone had scrawled on the sidewalk with yellow chalk: "Jesus lives!" Underneath that, someone had written, "Jesus is dead, Elvis lives."

Exactly, she thought.

EXODUS 32:1

> When the people saw that Moses delayed to come down from the mountain, the people gathered around Aaron, and said to him, "Come, make gods for us, who shall go before us."

STILL OURS

While eggs and bunnies appear in the store windows and tulips spell out "Happy Spring," it's not that easy to erase the figure of a tortured, would-be king whose wounds, even in resurrection, do not go away. The naked figure of a grown man dying on a cross defies coddling and doesn't do much for sales.

Easter is still ours!

ISAIAH 52:13-15

See, my servant shall prosper;
    He shall be exalted and lifted up,
    and shall be very high.
Just as there were many who were
      astonished at him
     –so marred was his appearance,
      beyond human semblance,
     and his form beyond that of mortals–
so shall he startle many nations.

SUMMER MAGIC

The old pastor had a big house, but it was already quite full when he took in another young man, a seminarian. Altogether there were six of them—two college students, two priests, the seminarian, and the pastor. They all sat at the long dining room table every evening eating and talking and laughing.

They all moved on at the end of the summer. The new pastor wanted to live alone and that was his right. In one of the serendipitous moments in their lives, they had been thrown together quite by accident. They knew as they packed their bags and said their goodbyes it had been a charmed summer.

Like the resurrection itself, it still breathes new life into each of them whenever it comes to mind.

JOHN 20:20-21

> Then the disciples rejoiced when they saw the Lord. Jesus said to them again, "Peace be with you. As the Father has sent me, so I send you."

Easter Joy

She clung to the righteousness of God, in whose justice everything certainly must be leveled out. A sin counter, she kept a ledger in case Saint Peter slipped up. Her sister was careless at prayer, ate candy during Lent, laughed in church at the new priest's jokes, owned a dress that fell above her knees, and talked to sinners. Oh, yes, she knew her sister's sins as well as she knew the Creed.

On Holy Thursday they kept the final hour of adoration before the Blessed Sacrament—she straight-backed and grim, her sister slouching and drowsy with a faint peaceful smile.

On Easter morning they lingered after Mass, adding prayers to the source and summit of the Christian life. Then they made the round of the sanctuary lilies, pulling out the yellow parts of the newly opened flowers—thereby preserving their virginity and insuring a longer life. As they left the church, she turned to her sister and, removing a speck of lint from her coat, said: "Happy Easter, dear." Her sister replied: "Happy Easter. I love you too."

The sun did not shine brighter, nor did peace break out in the world, but the balance of justice tipped in favor of redemption once again.

Psalm 118:24

This is the day that the Lord has made;
let us rejoice and be glad in it.

FRIENDSHIP

She was his oldest friend. They had met when they were only sixteen. Now she was about to enroll her daughter in the college where he taught. "I think she'll like it here," he said without ever thinking it would sound manipulative. "I mean, I think she'll do well here."

"I suppose you're right," she replied. "And you'll be close by to help her if she needs it."

"Oh, I doubt she'll need special help," he said, again never thinking she would judge that he didn't want to be bothered.

"She'll need it," she said. "Remember, I've lived with her for eighteen years. She's a handful."

"But she's grown up well," he countered. "There's so much of you in her."

She laughed. "Is that supposed to be a compliment?"

Of course it was supposed to be a compliment. She was one of the best people he knew. Whenever he was in trouble or depressed or in need of a kind ear, he always called her. "I don't tell you often enough what a good person you are, what a good friend you have been to me," he told her. "It has made a great difference in my life."

JOHN 15:12

> "This is my commandment, that you love one another as I have loved you."

FAITH

It was unbearable when they closed the casket of her ten-year-old. She slumped against her husband, who had to hold her up as he walked her back to the front pew. They sat together, holding each other during the funeral Mass.

At the cemetery, the priest read from one of the resurrection stories and then said to them, "As hard as this moment is, it is important to remember that your son is not here in this cold ground, and you should not think of him here. For he died with Christ in baptism and is now with the Lord. If you can remember that, this time and this place will not haunt you. Here you will find only one memory; do not let it be the memory that guides your days. You will find your son only by moving forward, for he has gone ahead of you."

Because she believed, this at last made sense to her.

LUKE 24:5

The women were terrified and bowed their faces to the ground, but the men said to them: "Why do you look for the living among the dead? He is not here, but has risen."

"FEED MY SHEEP"

A farming accident when he was thirteen stripped him of two fingers. His brothers went off to the war, but the army wouldn't take him because he wasn't whole. He stayed home and helped his father farm.

It took him fifty years to figure out that he, too, did something important during the war.

JOHN 21:15-17

When they had finished breakfast, Jesus said to Simon Peter, "Simon son of John, do you love me more than these?" He said to him, "Yes, Lord; you know that I love you." Jesus said to him, "Feed my lambs." A second time, he said to him, "Simon son of John, do you love me?" He said to him, "Yes, Lord; you know that I love you." Jesus said to him, "Tend my sheep." He said to him a third time, "Simon son of John, do you love me?" ...And he said to him, "Lord, you know everything; you know that I love you." Jesus said to him, "Feed my sheep."

The Asking

Sometimes we ask for too little to avoid being disappointed. While we are not disappointed, we are also not healed.

Acts 3:1-7

One day Peter and John were going up to the temple at the hour of prayer, at three o'clock in the afternoon. And a man lame from birth was being carried in . . . . When he saw Peter and John about to go into the temple, he asked them for alms. Peter looked intently at him, as did John, and said, "Look at us." And he fixed his attention on them, expecting to receive something from them. But Peter said, "I have no silver or gold, but what I have I give you; in the name of Jesus Christ of Nazareth, stand up and walk." And he took him by the right hand and raised him up; and immediately his feet and ankles were made strong.

Moving On

Sometimes when we are healed we cling to the cure as an end in itself, instead of moving on with our lives and becoming witnesses to God's love.

Acts 3:11

> While [the lame man] clung to Peter and John, all the people ran together to them in the portico called Solomon's Portico, utterly astonished.

APRIL SNOWSTORM

Shoveling the snow, he thought to himself, "This is April. I think I'm supposed to be doing something else."

His neighbor walked across the street and began helping him shovel. "I'm glad to help you," the neighbor said when he protested. "I've got my shoveling done already and I've already been to church."

Sometimes when we run away from the Lord, the Lord comes to find us—and we don't even recognize him.

LUKE 24:13-16

Now on that same day two of them were going to a village called Emmaus, about seven miles from Jerusalem, and talking with each other about all these things that had happened. While they were talking and discussing, Jesus himself came near and went with them, but their eyes were kept from recognizing him.

COMMUNITY LIFE

The nun was decidedly practical. If something needed doing, she found a way to do it. If an action was demanded by the gospel or her community, she pressed until it was done.

"Sometimes," she said, "That angers the good guys and sometimes it angers the bad guys. That's the funny thing about truth, there's always somebody on the other side of it looking at you."

JOHN 3:20-21

"For all who do evil hate the light and do not come to the light, so that their deeds may not be exposed. But those who do what is true come to the light, so that it may be clearly seen that their deeds have been done in God."

Fences

After he laid the new sod, he fenced it off so no one would walk on it. He stood back and admired his work and thought how wonderful it would be if his lawn always looked this good. His wife came out and handed him a glass of iced tea.

"Too bad," she said, pointing to the fence. "Grass is so much nicer to walk on than concrete."

Psalm 8:6

You have given them dominion over
the works of your hands;
you have put all things under
their feet.

The Fool

"Two in the rear," the woman announced with a high, squeaky giggle punctuated by a toss of her head and a light adjustment of her spangled glasses. She took her daughter's arm and together they paraded into the back room of the all-you-can-eat buffet restaurant.

She made a fuss of waiting for her chair to be pulled out and refused to settle in until the hostess had placed a chair under her daughter in just the right position. "What shall we have, honey?" she asked in a shrill voice that everyone could hear. "Well, I guess we'll have the buffet." And she laughed and laughed and laughed at her own joke.

She insisted loudly on going to the buffet for her daughter."This is your day, honey; let Mommy serve you." Each trip through the buffet line was a parody of discretion and good taste. She became the topic of conversation at every table.

Because of the woman's antics, no one really noted the daughter's disabilities. Nor did anyone notice how the child beamed with delight at the mother who would sacrifice even her dignity for her little girl.

1 Corinthians 1:27

> God chose what is foolish in the world to shame the wise.

WISDOM

The woman had been born to poor immigrants who couldn't afford to send her to school but did what they could for her, teaching her to read from the Bible. She had the humility of Mother Teresa —and all the spunk as well. She never had to raise her voice to make her point and never resorted to manipulation to get her way.

The girl at the convenience store checkout counter, after hearing her broken English, placed the change in her hand slowly, counting each penny, nickel, and dime. The woman had to laugh. The team of accountants in the company she owned had never been so careful with her money.

MARK 6:2

On the sabbath he began to teach in the synagogue, and many who heard him were astounded. They said, "Where did this man get all this? What is this wisdom that has been given to him?"

In Vain

He had a funny way of swearing, using all sorts of contorted and contrived words to avoid the real ones he was thinking. He thought that if he didn't say the actual words he wasn't using God's name in vain.

ACTS 4:12

"There is salvation in no one else, for there is no other name under heaven given among mortals by which we must be saved."

THE GROCER

There were two grocery stores in town run by the same man. The one in the better part of town sold only the finest produce. When it didn't sell fast enough and began to wither, the man shipped it across town to the other store, raised the price on it, and sold it to the poor people.

PSALM 113:5-8

Who is like the LORD our God,
    who is seated on high,
who looks far down
    on the heavens and the earth?
He raises the poor from the dust,
    and lifts the needy from the ash heap,
to make them sit with princes,
    with the princes of his people.

IMAGES

He could never understand how people saw images of Jesus in the oddest places: on the sides of mountains and barns, the creases of old cloth, misshapen pieces of driftwood, swirls of paint on billboards, and granite tombstones. All these inanimate objects showing forth the Lord seemed to him to be a distraction from the task of looking for God in more lively places.

LUKE 21:25-28

"There will be signs in the sun, the moon, and the stars, and on the earth distress among nations confused by the roaring of the sea and the waves. People will faint from fear and foreboding of what is coming upon the world, for the powers of the heavens will be shaken. Then they will see 'the Son of Man coming in a cloud' with power and great glory. Now when these things begin to take place, stand up and raise your heads, because your redemption is drawing near."

THE INHERITANCE

He didn't remember ever missing Sunday Mass
when he was a child. It was as much a part of the
routine in his parents' home as the Saturday night
bath and Sunday morning Polish sausage. There
was never a question about going to church. It just
happened.

His great-great-grandfather on his father's side
had dug the church foundation with a team of
horses. It took an entire summer. Every time he
went down into the basement for a funeral luncheon or a wedding feast, he was within inches of
the sweat of that man. Every time he knelt at the
communion rail, the expectations of his ancestors
rose in his throat and clung to the roof of his
mouth.

ACTS 4:31

When they had prayed, the place in
which they were gathered together was
shaken; and they were all filled with
the Holy Spirit and spoke the word of
God with boldness.

THE OLD FARMSTEAD

They drove past the farm where his mother had grown up. Her father had been a sheep herder, dairy farmer, and logger. Later that evening, his mother showed him pictures of her great-grandfather riding one of the first tractors in the area. "A silly old thing with two speeds: too slow and too fast. It was useless, but he was proud of it," she laughed.

They drove past the cemetery where those giants of his personal history were buried, then to a small town where he used to watch the American Legion baseball teams play.

Back at his parents' home, they dined on potatoes, cabbage, and farm-grown chicken. For dessert there were the last of the strawberries his mother had frozen the summer before.

He hoped never to grow so old or go so far from his childhood that he wouldn't be able to enjoy this peasants' feast.

JOHN 3:4

Nicodemus said to him, "How can anyone be born after having grown old?

THE HAY MOW

She had a shy smile on a mouth too small for her teeth. Her hair was the color and texture of straw. She wasn't a pretty child, but her bright blue eyes combined sadness and hope in twin sparkles.

Three days after her sixteenth birthday, the oldest son of the farmer next door brought back a hay wagon his father had borrowed. She walked him to the hay mow where they spent fifteen minutes alone. She didn't really understand what had happened, but her cheeks were brighter than they'd ever been before and her eyes had lost a trace of their sadness.

Nine months later, after the boy had moved to the city to get a factory job, she delivered a baby girl. She called her Enola, which is "Alone" spelled backwards.

The woman has a grandson now who has a real name, John. She holds him on her knees and rubs his nose to hers. She speaks softly to him and reminds him as often as she can: "John, if you ever go to the hay mow with a girl, be sure to give her your address when you move away."

2 CORINTHIANS 1:3-4

Blessed be the God and Father of our Lord Jesus Christ, the Father of mercies and the God of all consolation, who consoles us all in our affliction, so that we may be able to console those who are in any affliction with the consolation with which we ourselves are consoled by God.

THE FUNERAL

The woman pointed to where the old lady used to sit. "You remember her, don't you, honey?" she asked her seven-year-old daughter. "She always wore floppy hats. I'm sure you remember her." But for all her mother's coaxing, the little girl could not.

When no funeral was announced, the woman questioned the pastor. He said the family had decided on a private kind of farewell.

The woman took her daughter's hand and led her to the statue of the Sacred Heart. She put in a dollar and had the child light a candle.

LUKE 1:50

"His mercy is for those who fear him
from generation to generation."

TULIPS

Looking at the tulips that were just coming up, she could almost see the color they would bring to her front yard. She wondered if there would be flowers on the banquet table of heaven.

JOHN 3:12

"If I have told you about earthly things and you do not believe, how can you believe if I tell you about heavenly things?"

SOLUTIONS

She was wise enough to know that all of her problems wouldn't be solved this side of heaven. So she did the best she could with what she had.

PSALM 34:19

Many are the afflictions of the
  righteous,
    but the LORD rescues them from
    them all.

CHEWING GUM CRITIC

One Sunday, when his parents brought him to church in a navy sailor suit, the little boy came chanting a new song in grim determination to obtain more chewing gum: "Gum, gum, gum! Gum, gum! Gum, gum, gum! Gum, gum!"

After a great deal of shushing, his parents parceled out small bits of chewing gum to him, tearing thin sticks into tiny slivers in the hope they would have enough to last through Mass.

Just as the priest had gotten to the main point of his homily, the boy yelled for more gum. By this time his mouth was so full that it came out, "Dumb, dumb, dumb! Dumb, dumb!"

Someone in the assembly began applauding, and the entire congregation joined in enthusiastically—the priest among them.

ACTS 6:7

The word of God continued to spread;
the number of the disciples increased
greatly in Jerusalem, and a great many of
the priests became obedient to the faith.

Drawn by the Father

It wasn't until he gave up trying so hard that he
actually heard the Lord speak to him in prayer.

John 6:44

"No one can come to me unless
drawn by the Father who sent me;
and I will raise that person up on the
last day."

FOOL'S GOLD

Winter hung on far too long the year she moved north to Minnesota. The gray, cold days plodded along, one after another, like nineteenth-century coal miners going to work. She was sure spring would come; it had to come—even here. Didn't it?

She found a dandelion on her way to work and wondered if it was fool's gold.

JOHN 10:22-24

It was winter, and Jesus was walking in the temple, in the portico of Solomon. So the Jews gathered around him and said to him, "How long will you keep us in suspense?"

To the Giver

Even as a child who believed in Santa Claus, he had trouble looking beyond the gift to the giver.

John 12:44

Then Jesus cried aloud: "Whoever believes in me believes not in me but in him who sent me."

THE GROTTO

At sixty-five, two years after retiring because one leg had gone gimpy, the priest began hauling stones to a pile on the convent lawn. The sisters had counted on him these past two years to drive them wherever they needed to go. Not wanting to offend their "chauffeur," they just watched in wonder as he stacked more and more stones against the hillside separating their home from his rectory. Finally, they sent the youngest sister out to him. She asked quietly, avoiding his deep brown eyes, "What are you doing with all these stones, Father?"

He said, "I'm building a grotto for Our Lady." The young sister, reverting for a moment to pre-convent manners, blurted out, "But where is Our Lady?" The priest smiled. "She'll be along shortly."

For days, the sisters watched as he hauled, piled, set, and reset stones into a free-standing alcove and then into a terraced garden planted with petunias. When he finished, there was still no statue of Our Lady in the grotto . . . only the promise that she would appear shortly.

LUKE 1:46-49

"My soul magnifies the Lord,
    and my spirit rejoices in God my Savior,
for he has looked with favor on the lowliness of
        his servant.
    Surely, from now on all generations will call
        me blessed;
for the Mighty One has done great things for me,
    and holy is his name.

HANDOUT

As he rang the rectory doorbell, he was careful not to appear too threatening. When the young priest came to the door, he simply said: "I need some money for food. If you could see your way clear to give me some, I would sure appreciate it."

The young priest reached into his trouser pocket and pulled out two singles. "This is all I have right now," he said.

The man accepted the money, knowing the priest was lying.

MATTHEW 13:14

> "You will indeed listen, but never understand,
>   and you will indeed look, but never perceive."

Evening Prayer

As she went to bed, she prayed that tomorrow would be a better day. And in case it wasn't, she prayed for the strength to live through it.

"Do not let your hearts be troubled.
Believe in God, believe also in me."

Traffic Stop

He stopped his car in the middle of a busy street, got out, and went across the median to the driver of a car going in the opposite direction. "Thank you," he said. "I'll never forget what you did for us. I'll never forget your kindness." Then he got back into his car and drove off.

The traffic, momentarily halted for this humble expression of gratitude, began to move again.

Luke 17:17-18

> "Were not ten made clean? But the other nine, where are they? Was none of them found to return and give praise to God except this foreigner?"

ONLY HUMAN

Even as a child, she had trouble differentiating between the things of God and God. Now that she was angry at the Church, she had stopped believing in God altogether.

ACTS 14:14-15

When the apostles Barnabas and Paul heard of it, they tore their clothes and rushed out into the crowd, shouting, "Friends, why are you doing this? We are mortals just like you, and we bring you good news, that you should turn from these worthless things to the living God, who made the heaven and the earth and the sea and all that is in them."

His Final Act

Three qualities made him the ideal chief of the town's volunteer fire department: he never went anywhere, he was a sucker for lost causes, and people trusted him. For twenty years, he supervised Fourth of July fireworks; put out brush, barn, and house fires; and pulled stray cats out of trees.

The entire town turned out for his funeral on a windy day in May. The fire department brought the truck to the church to carry his body to the cemetery. As the priest began the committal service, a gust of wind tore a tent pole from the nearly frozen ground. The tent collapsed in a fury. No one was hit by the flying pole, but the casket was knocked off its moorings.

It was the most excitement he had caused in his entire life.

Judith 10:17

> There was great excitement in the camp.

Obsessed

To be nothing less than obsessed with God—no matter how out of the ordinary it may seem—is the only true response to God's goodness.

PSALM 70:4

Let all who seek you
    rejoice and be glad in you.
Let those who love your salvation
    say evermore, "God is great!"

On the El

It was her first time in Chicago and her first time on the El. Everyone knew she was from Iowa because she wore a cap with Iowa written in red chaser lights hooked up to a battery pack. They also knew because of the way she gawked, fascinated with everything. She broke the El's etiquette by looking at people and smiling.

She had boarded with three boys, all of them at least fifty years younger than she was. They must have been her grandsons, for they had her freckles and square face. They stood around her like palace guards.

She wanted to walk the length of the train and look out the front windows. The boys tried to stop her, but it was impossible. "I know where I've been," she said to them, "I want to see where I'm going." She winked at a man about her age.

MATTHEW 18:3

> "Truly I tell you, unless you change
> and become like children, you will
> never enter the kingdom of heaven."

FAMILY GATHERINGS

He was always out of the family circle. Whenever they gathered, he would remain silent or go hunting in the fridge for something to nibble on. When they spoke of the old days growing up in their household, he would look preoccupied, pretending not to hear. Even when one of his children questioned him rather than their mother, who always dominated the conversations, he just smiled and nodded or shook his head.

He had been this way since his brother died. He could no longer believe that, as good as the good old days had been, the future was even brighter.

Unable to forgive God for his loss, his anger had turned to withdrawal.

JOHN 12:40

"He has blinded their eyes
    and hardened their heart,
so that they might not look with their
    eyes,
    and understand with their heart
    and turn—
and I would heal them."

JOY

When she could not give someone good news,
she said nothing. Her discretion was not a burden
but some sort of grace that made her cheeks rosy
and her touch healing.

JOHN 15:11

"I have said these things to you so
that my joy may be in you, and that
your joy may be complete."

Morning People

She would not allow her children to be grumpy at the table in the morning. It wasn't just good manners, it was a sense of responsibility for the beginning of a new day. "If you're going to mope and harp on your sister or brother," she would say, "you are not fit to receive the gift God is giving you this morning."

All her children married morning people who smiled before breakfast.

Psalm 57:8-9

Awake, my soul!
Awake, O harp and lyre!
    I will awake the dawn.
I will give thanks to you, O Lord, among
    the peoples.

BEARING FRUIT

He finally realized that praying was something he did not for his own good but for the good of the world.

JOHN 15:16
_____

> "And I appointed you to go and bear fruit, fruit that will last, so that the Father will give you whatever you ask in my name."

AND THE ANGELS SING

She died in her sleep. She wasn't sick; she was just old. One of the sisters found her when she didn't show up for morning prayers. After someone called the funeral director, all the sisters in the house came to her room and stood outside her doorway. One of them began singing and the others joined in. They didn't stop until the funeral director took her away.

It is possible these were the voices of angels, and it is possible that in community life there is the foretaste and the promise of heaven.

MATTHEW 24:30-31

"Then the sign of the Son of Man will appear in heaven, and then all the tribes of the earth will mourn, and they will see 'the Son of Man coming on the clouds of heaven' with power and great glory. And he will send out his angels with a loud trumpet call, and they will gather his elect from the four winds, from one end of heaven to the other."

Discipline

The children rarely did what she asked. She commanded, screamed, threatened, cajoled, nursed, bribed—to no avail.

But when their father spoke, they did what he asked without hesitation.

The difference, their father pointed out, was that their mother sounded as if *she* would die if they didn't do what she asked. When he spoke, he made it sound as if *they* would die if they didn't.

Ephesians 6:1-4

Children, obey your parents in the Lord, for this is right. "Honor your father and mother"–this is the first commandment with a promise: "so that it may be well with you and you may live long on the earth." And, fathers, do not provoke your children to anger, but bring them up in the discipline and instruction of the Lord.

GIFT AND GIVER

Often what comes to us as pure gift is taken from someone else. We think it is God's doing, and it may be, but it may also be someone else's sacrifice.

MARK 4:24-25

And he said to them, "Pay attention to what you hear; the measure you give will be the measure you get, and still more will be given you. For to those who have, more will be given; and from those who have nothing, even what they have will be taken away."

The Mustache

He started growing the mustache because, well, because he forgot to shave his upper lip one Sunday morning. And when he got ready for work on Monday, he thought it didn't look bad. At first everyone gave him a hard time about it, but eventually the talk died down.

After ten years with the mustache, he shaved it off on another Sunday morning because, well, because he made a big swipe on the right side of it with his razor. He couldn't go into work with half a mustache and he couldn't make up a story to cover what he'd done without looking foolish.

When he went to work on Monday, everyone asked about the missing mustache. He was momentarily speechless, and then it just came to him: "I promised that if God would help me quit smoking, I'd shave off my mustache."

It had never occurred to him to quit smoking until now. Maybe God was . . . nah, that would be *too* spooky.

<u>Romans 11:33</u>

> O the depth of the riches and wisdom and knowledge of God! How unsearchable are his judgments and how inscrutable his ways!

MARY'S CORNER

She felt out of sync. Didn't her friends understand how much pain there is in the world? How could they go on pretending nothing was wrong when nothing was as it should be?

She went to church and prayed, not for her friends but for the world in which they all lived. She saw the statue of Mary in the corner with only one votive candle lit. She dropped all the money she had on her into the slot and lit all the candles.

"You listen because you know," she said to the woman behind the image. "You know we don't live the way your Son intended us to live."

JOHN 16:20

"Very truly, I tell you, you will weep
and mourn, but the world will
rejoice; you will have pain, but your
pain will turn into joy."

Already Loved

She wasted a lot of time trying to earn her father's respect, when all she really wanted was to know he loved her.

John 16:27

> "The Father himself loves you,
> because you have loved me and have
> believed that I came from God."

Pastoral Naps

His first spiritual director in the seminary told him he would never be ordained because he was a pragmatist who acted not out of principle but out of accommodation.

Ordained now many years, the priest admits to the accommodation, saying, "I don't know how else to keep my balance in a Church that—though built on an ancient rock—trembles and shifts according to the most current spiritual paradigm."

So, after every ordination he goes back to his rectory and gets ready for the future by taking a pastoral nap.

Pastoral naps graciously pass the time between paradigm shifts.

MATTHEW 16:18

"And I tell you, you are Peter, and on this rock I will build my church, and the gates of Hades will not prevail against it."

THE PRISONER

He spent time in a federal halfway house, a quasi-prison for people who didn't pay their taxes. While there, he could go to work every day, not in the bar he used to run but in a more acceptable kind of job. There was no getting out early for good behavior, which he surely exhibited. The best thing that happened to him was that he stopped drinking.

He became a new man, not because of the crime but because of the punishment.

PSALM 68:6

> God gives the desolate a home to live in;
> > he leads out the prisoners to
> > > prosperity,
> > but the rebellious live in a parched
> > land.

PLAIN TALK

She didn't exactly hear God's voice, but the day the oncoming car missed her by inches she suddenly realized how precious life was. She wasn't going to waste any more of it.

God didn't have to hit her over the head twice for her to get the message.

JOHN 16:29

His disciples said, "Yes, now you are speaking plainly, not in any figure of speech!"

BITS OF TRUTH

They were the arbiters of class and distinction in their small town. They assumed their influence by the willful use of gossip: a softly spoken word to the neighbor hanging out the laundry, a confidential clasp of the hand in the grocery store, feigned embarrassment at a PTA meeting, sympathetic nodding outside of Sunday Mass. They didn't lie, but they used tiny bits of truth with long and often silent intervals of inference to maintain the social network as they saw it or believed it should be. They were best at exhibiting horrified astonishment when their little bits of truth came back to them magnified and solidified.

On this particular Sunday, these two ladies take up positions outside the church. The gospel of the day is about the woman caught in adultery. They have little bits of truth to tell, but they keep it to themselves for now.

There is always the possibility that the gospel might be true.

WISDOM 1:11

> Beware then of useless grumbling,
> and keep your tongue from slander;
> because no secret word is without result,
> and a lying mouth destroys the soul.

A Conundrum

He always wondered whether it was supposed to be, "What's good for you is good for your neighbor" or "What's good for your neighbor is good for you."

Who was supposed to come first, him or his neighbor?

Each of us must please our neighbor
for the good purpose of building up
the neighbor.

What's in a Name?

Names used to be given as something to live up to or someone to look up to, passed down in families like treasures. Today, almost no one wants to name their children after anyone.

Too bad. There are a lot of good people out there to be emulated

John 17:11

> "Holy Father, protect them in your name that you have given me, so that they may be one, as we are one."

Second Thoughts

"Are you sure you want to do that?" his father would say. Eventually, the son learned that the question deserved careful consideration.

He read somewhere that, "God is found in our second thoughts—between the spark of desire or thought and any one of our actions to fulfill the desire or complete the thought."

Second thoughts are what distinguish us from animals. Second thoughts may, in fact, be how we are made in the image and likeness of God.

Proverbs 2:1-5

My child, if you accept my words
    and treasure up my commandments
        within you,
making your ear attentive to wisdom
    and inclining your heart to
        understanding;
if you indeed cry out for insight,
    and raise your voice for
        understanding;
if you seek it like silver,
    and search for it as for hidden
        treasures—
then you will understand the fear of
    the Lord
    and find the knowledge of God.

THE QUESTION

Her face slumped almost beyond recognition after he asked her, "Do you love me—yes or no?" She never dreamed he would ask the question in such a way that she couldn't lie.

JOHN 21:15
_____

When they had finished breakfast, Jesus said to Simon Peter, "Simon son of John, do you love me more than these?"

THE RED BIRD

She liked to imagine that her dead daughter was a cardinal, a red bird that came and made a home in her backyard for the summers. She didn't really believe that her daughter was a bird, but she did know that somehow her daughter was not totally lost to her now that she was dead. She reasoned, "If those early Christians could imagine the Holy Spirit as a dove hovering over their everyday cares and woes and joys, why can't my precious daughter be a cardinal? They couldn't believe that Jesus would desert them, I can't believe my daughter would be gone forever."

JOHN 15:26-27

"When the Advocate comes, whom I will send to you from the Father, the Spirit of truth who comes from the Father, he will testify on my behalf. You also are to testify because you have been with me from the beginning."

KNOWLEDGE AND WISDOM

He had a photographic memory. He read the Bible from cover to cover when he was in the sixth and seventh grades. He spent grades eight through eleven reading every volume of the encyclopedia.

When he finished reading all there was to know about this world and the next, he still couldn't figure out which was the most important.

LUKE 10:41-42

> "Martha, Martha, you are worried and distracted by many things; there is need of only one thing."

ONLY MONEY

He thought that when he retired he would work in a homeless shelter or soup kitchen. He would finally live up to the words he often told his children, "It's *only* money."

However, the day after he retired an old friend offered him a job selling used trucks, which he did for a while, saving the commissions he earned. For what, he did not know.

He quit the job after six months and did what he knew he should have been doing all along.

JOHN 14:12

"Very truly, I tell you, the one who believes in me will also do the works that I do."

Wee Wisdom

As he pulled weeds with his mother in the family garden, he asked, "Where do weeds come from, Mom?"

"They're good plants gone bad," said his mother quickly.

"Were there weeds in the beginning?" he asked.

"In the beginning?" she said, "What do you mean, in the beginning?"

"You know," he said, "in that garden by Eden?"

His mother smiled, "No, there weren't any weeds, then," she said. "Everything was good."

"Did these weeds forget how to be good?"

"I suppose," she said, still smiling.

"Shouldn't we give them a chance to be good again?" he asked with a naively sly insistence.

Psalm 19:7

The law of the LORD is perfect,
  reviving the soul;
the decrees of the LORD are sure,
  making wise the simple.

BERRY PICKING

In public parks we are forbidden to pick the flowers for our pleasure, but no one seems to mind if we eat the berries that grow on prickly stalks.

MATTHEW 7:16

"You will know them by their fruits. Are grapes gathered from thorns, or figs from thistles?"

Cousins

The name of the reporter on TV caught her attention. It was her grandmother's last name. "I wonder if we're related?" she thought to herself.

It is an indulgence common to all humanity: we are always on the lookout for lost relatives. Our last name in a phone book or newspaper article catches our eye and we wonder anew.

It may take more than these chance encounters to discover our lost cousins; it may take faith that we are related to more people than we could ever imagine.

Genesis 15:5

> He brought him outside and said, "Look toward heaven and count the stars, if you are able to count them." Then he said to him, "So shall your descendants be."

THE RUNAWAY

When he was eleven, he ran and hid in the hollowed-out stump of a great white pine. There he felt safe, even though he had neither food nor plan. He was breathing heavily from running when his older brother came to drag him home.

This older brother was not as bright as he, but he was slightly bigger. "If you don't come home right now, you're going to get a licking."

"I will anyway," the boy shot back.

"Just get out of there and come back with me," yelled the older brother. He hauled him out of the stump and dragged him back home.

Now sixty-two, the man still bears the scars of that morning and does not smile when his brother tells the story. Going home is rarely as easy as the Wizard of Oz made it sound.

LUKE 15:20

"So he set off and went to his father. But while he was still far off, his father saw him and was filled with compassion."

THE TOUCH

She sits by the front door, on the concrete patio her husband built. "I miss my Ted," she says to the two men who sit with backs to the sun, drinking iced tea.

One of them responds. "I met him only a few times, but I could see he was a good man and I could see he loved you."

She flashes a smile which turns to a grimace. "It's the touching I miss most." She flicks the tips of her fingers against her thumbs. "I miss how he felt."

She adjusts her straw hat as sprinkles of sunlight fall on her face and she looks away to some memory of him coming across the concrete to kiss her.

PSALM 112:6

For the righteous will never be
    moved;
      they will be remembered forever.

EXPRESSION

He has a look of permanent surprise. When he was young, it misled his teachers into thinking he was slow. Today it teases colleagues into telling him tales. He plays along. "No? Really? Are you sure?" he says with his expression.

On Sundays, sitting next to his daughter at church, he listens intently to the word of God. The incredulity on his face draws the attention of those who thought they already knew how the story turned out.

JEREMIAH 15:16

Your words were found, and I ate them,
    Your words became to me a joy
    and the delight of my heart;
for I am called by your name,
    O LORD, God of hosts.

Clouds

They lie on their backs and point to the clouds. They see sailing ships and dragons, bears and petunias, all rising out of amorphous fluff and foundering against a perfect blue sky. These creations, not entirely of their own imagining and not entirely sensible, absolutely and perfectly belong only to this time and place . . . and to the two of them.

Like the fondness between them, these things would not exist had they not taken the time to look.

PSALM 25:5

Lead me in your truth, and teach me,
for you are the God of my
salvation;
for you I wait all day long.

Flight Insurance

She was surprised to hear his voice on the answering machine. She had just dropped him off at the airport.

"I just wanted you to know I bought flight insurance," he said. "It's the deluxe package so I'm covered all the while I am traveling."

Recalling the last smile on his face, she erases the message . . . and then immediately regrets it.

2 Timothy 1:4

Recalling your tears, I long to see
you so that I may be filled with joy.

WEDDING PICTURE

She remembers the magnet on her mother's refrigerator door—a rainbow with the words: "God made us and God doesn't make junk." When she was thirteen and feeling particularly awkward and unlovable, she would read it and sneer. At twenty-three, she knew she was ugly. There is no likeness of her in any scrapbook that pleases her eye.

But now, as she poses for her wedding picture, her arm around the man she has just promised to love "forever," she is more hopeful that the words of the magnet may be true.

WISDOM 19:18

> For the elements changed places with
>   one another,
> as on a harp the notes vary the nature
>   of the rhythm,
> while each note remains the same.

First Person

They were walking through the first forty acres of forest his father had ever purchased. Finally the boy said, "Do you think anyone else has ever been here?"

His father laughed. "Of course. We bought this land from old Guy Warner."

"Well, maybe old Guy Warner," the boy said with insistence, " but not anyone else, for sure."

Again his father laughed. "Well, of course, other people. Guy Warner got it from some Civil War colonel."

"So we're like the second and third people ever to see this?" he asked hopefully.

"Sure," said his father, hoping to put an end to the conversation.

The boy dug deep into the soil with the toe of his shoe, pulling up black leaves first, then mossy stuff, then rich black earth. "I bet I'm the first person to see this," he said, pointing to the bottom of the hole.

"Sure," his father said over his shoulder. "Except for God."

Psalm 123:1

To you I lift up my eyes,
    O you who are enthroned in the heavens!

THE CONCERT

She scribbled the note on her program and sent it back with one of the ushers. "Do you remember me?" the note read. "I was your first piano student, forty years ago." She had signed her name and was now embarrassed at having sent it.

As she was leaving the concert hall, the usher handed her a note. It read, "Mary, meet me by the stage door in twenty minutes. We have some catching up to do."

LUKE 19:5

When Jesus came to the place, he
looked up and said to him,
"Zacchaeus, hurry and come down;
for I must stay at your house today."

State Fair

They were walking through the livestock barns at a local fair. It struck her that her thirty-year-old son was actually enjoying himself. "How did this happen?" she asked him.

Leaning over a pen to look more closely at a calf, he responded, "How did what happen?"

"How is it that you are actually enjoying this? I remember when you were fifteen, you threw a fit when I wanted to take you to the fair."

"When I was fifteen," he said, straightening up and putting his arm around her, "I didn't want anyone to know I had parents."

Like learning to acknowledge our parents at thirty, maybe it takes time to learn to believe in the God we discarded when we were fifteen.

2 Timothy 3:14-15

But as for you, continue in what you have learned and firmly believed, knowing from whom you learned it, and how from childhood you have known the sacred writings that are able to instruct you for salvation through faith in Christ Jesus.

Freeway Flapper

With apparent clarity of purpose, unswayable determination, and awkward grace, she flapped, flapped, flapped across the freeway overpass.

A tide of cars slowed to watch her singular procession and then accelerated to make up for the scattered seconds of lost time. Fathers and mothers pointed as their children craned forward across seat backs. Business men and women laid their cell phones aside; truck drivers honked and mobile munchers paused in mid-bite. Why would this woman don full snorkeling gear miles from water and make a public spectacle of herself? Was it a bid for attention? Did she have a great sense of humor? Had she lost a bet? Was she an alien, newly landed and unsure of this planet's life support system?

The harder we try to place this woman's conduct in a logical framework, the less likely we are to come to a conclusion.

Romans 9:25
_____

"Those who were not my people I
will call 'my people,'
and her who was not beloved I will
call 'beloved.'"

Embarrassment

Every weekend, she came to church proudly with her parents, her golden hair in braids or brushed and fluffy, her smile as wide as her five-year-old face. This weekend, however, a childish hat covered her hair and a cloud covered her face. When the priest greeted her, she didn't respond. "What's the matter?" he asked. Silence.

"C'mon," he cajoled, "You can tell me." Her hand shot up to her mouth, muffling her mumbled response. "I'm sorry," he said, "I didn't quite catch that." Hand still in place, she mumbled a little louder. "It might help if you take your hand away from your mouth," the priest pointed out gently. A look of childish terror steamed red onto the little girl's face. She ran to a dark corner of the church.

"What's wrong with her?" the priest asked her mother.

"She lost her four front teeth this week."

"But that's not so bad," said the priest, "everyone loses teeth."

The mother just shook her head. "She just doesn't know that yet."

WISDOM 6:17

The beginning of wisdom is the sincere desire for instruction.

Procrastination

He went out early to water the lawn. As he stretched the hose, it kinked behind him. He wished he had done a better job rolling it up the last time he used it.

He spent a lot of time putting off doing things the right way, hoping the consequences of his procrastination would disappear. They never did and he never learned.

On this bright June morning, as he struggled to get the kinks out of the hose, he was once again optimistic that he could change.

Sirach 43:8

> The new moon, as its name suggest,
> renews itself;
> how marvelous it is in this change!

THE BRIDESMAID

She had never been able to wear "girl clothes" well. When she was born, her legs were all scrunched behind her and came out at the same time her head did. The doctor warned her parents that she might never walk right and the angles of her body would seem wrong at first glance.

When she was asked to stand up for her friend's wedding, she was thrilled. They took pictures in front of the altar, where a large crucifix dominated the sanctuary. Jesus would be in the picture with them, his broken and contorted body somehow a balm for the cross she bore all her life.

In the final wedding pictures, it was her smile that everyone noticed.

MATTHEW 5:8

"Blessed are the pure in heart,
for they will see God."

Father Love

On the phone, their voices all sounded like their father's—voices that even at a young age seemed to reach way down in their stomachs. They had his speech patterns, too: short quips, smart aleck comments, belly laughs. They, like him, had hearts a mile wide. They assumed all people liked them because they liked all people.

On Father's Day, they drew their own stocky images on a card. Inside they wrote, "We're the best gift we can give you." He pulled them all to him and hugged them all at once, squeezing something more of himself into each of them.

And he understood in that moment how God could love the world into being.

PSALM 4:6-7

> There are many who say, "O that we
> might see some good!
> Let the light of your face shine on
> us, O LORD!"
> You have put gladness in my heart
> more than when their grain and
> wine abound.

Handles on Sandwiches

He believed every sandwich had a handle. The rest of the world could nibble the last crumb of a hamburger or ham and Swiss, but not him. He knew that once you grab hold of the bread, you have found a handle and have identified that piece of the universe for good purpose. To him, it was as natural and explicitly pragmatic as reaching for the hilt of a sword rather than its blade.

His friends chided him for the compressed bits of bread, cheese, lettuce, and meats he always left on his plate. "You're wasting food," they said.

He was undeterred. "This," he said, holding up the pinched deli remains, "is not food. It is a handle, and handles are not meant for eating."

His friends would shake their heads and admit, in their more reflective moments, that he was able to see things they could not.

MATTHEW 13:17

"Truly I tell you, many prophets and righteous people longed to see what you see, but did not see it, and to hear what you hear, but did not hear it."

ALONE

The old nun walked because her doctor said it was good for her; it made her blood flow better and kept her weight down so her knees would last longer.

She walked because out here in the country there was more silence than in her convent.

She walked because then she could be alone, and sometimes it was easier to have faith when it wasn't being tested by the fact that God expected her to love her sisters as herself.

LUKE 10:27

"You shall love the Lord your God with all your heart, and with all your soul, and with all your strength, and with all your mind; and your neighbor as yourself."

GOD'S VINEYARD

At eighty, he was through with long trips. He had seen the world, met the pope, ate in a Belgrade restaurant, and then dispersed the family fortune among his children and worthy causes.

When his wife died three years ago, he tore up both of their passports. He was going to see what he had missed right here where he lived: the long stand of oaks that lined one of the prettiest streets in America, the new sewage plant that made the river cleaner, the restored train depot. He visited these places in his hometown over and over and was thrilled anew each time he went.

"God's vineyard is as wide as the world," he would say to his children, "and as close as your back-yard."

PSALM 16:11

You show me the path of life.
In your presence there is
fullness of joy;
in your right hand are
pleasures forevermore.

Matching Coats

For their anniversary he bought her a leather coat and a matching one for himself. His teenage children couldn't believe their father had done such a thing. They were embarrassed for him.

His wife understood. She was wise enough to know that to "become one" takes a lot of trial and error.

Matthew 19:5

"For this reason a man shall leave his father and mother and be joined to his wife, and the two shall become one flesh."

Extra Time

The last vacation they all took together was to Yellowstone. They got back three days early and the parents couldn't have been happier. The children didn't understand this happiness and, in fact, felt a little gypped. Their father tried to explain: "But now we have all this extra time."

When you're a child, there is always extra time. Extra time doesn't mean anything, except when you wheedle ten more minutes out of your parents at bedtime.

Adults understand extra time. It's time no one has a claim on; it's extra because you didn't schedule anything during it. Extra time doesn't happen much anymore. Everything is premeasured and pre-mixed, accounted for before it's spent or sold or used up.

We need extra time to remind us of God's grace and to teach us what it might be like to delight in eternity—which is *all* extra time.

Ecclessiastes 3:1

For everything there is a season,
and a time for every matter
under heaven.

Born to Teach

She was a born teacher who helped even the most difficult children learn, but last June she decided to try something different. She signed up for a real estate course. She thought she could make money just by being nice to people and honest with them. She liked the idea of driving around all day, looking at homes, and being able to take a day off without feeling guilty.

By October, however, she missed the children and the regularity of classroom schedules. She missed those twenty-five tiny horizons growing disproportionately and surprisingly.

She missed doing what she was best at—maybe even what she was put on this earth to do.

2 Corinthians 6:1-2

> As we work together with him, we urge you also not to accept the grace of God in vain. For he says, "At an acceptable time I have listened to you, and on a day of salvation I have helped you."

THE BARGAIN

She was just at the stage where she not only knew her own will but knew how to pester her mother into fulfilling it. "This is a nice wagon, isn't it, Mommy?

"Yes, it's a nice wagon, honey," her mother agreed.

"I can have this wagon, can't I, Mommy?"

"Not today, honey. It costs too much money."

"But I really, really want this wagon, Mommy."

"I said, we don't have enough money to buy the wagon today."

"How about a candy bar, Mommy?"

"Yes, we have enough money for a candy bar."

When we bargain with God, do we start out asking for the sun and the moon . . . when what we really want is God's love?

ROMANS 8:26-27

Likewise the Spirit helps us in our weakness; for we do not know how to pray as we ought, but that very Spirit intercedes with sighs too deep for words. And God, who searches the heart, knows what is the mind of the Spirit, because the Spirit intercedes for the saints according to the will of God.

INSIDE STUFF

Years ago, when she left the convent, he bought her a wallet with compartments for cash and a checkbook. "You'll need this," he had said.

She replied, "You goose, I don't have either cash or a checking account."

"But you'll get them," he insisted.

"I suppose," was all she said.

Twenty years later, when they met for lunch, he thought she hadn't changed much from then. To be sure, her hair was gray and she had put on weight and she had wrinkles; but the stuff inside hadn't changed. And then she pulled out the wallet he had purchased for her so many years before. "I can't believe you're still using that thing," he said.

She giggled, "When you don't use something very often, you don't wear it out."

2 CORINTHIANS 4:5-6

For we do not proclaim ourselves; we proclaim Jesus Christ as Lord and ourselves as your slaves for Jesus' sake. For it is God who said, "Let light shine out of darkness," who has shone in our hearts to give the light of the knowledge of the glory of God in the face of Jesus Christ.

THE BUS DRIVER

Today a miracle happened. A city bus driver actually backed up her bus to pick up an old man. The man was so tired from running to catch the bus he just couldn't walk the last few feet to board it. When she told her husband how she had violated every rule in the transit authority's rule book to do it, he asked her why.

All she could say was, "I don't know. It was like God just wanted this one little thing done."

MATTHEW 5:42

"Give to everyone who begs from you, and do not refuse anyone."

GENERATION

He held his day-old son as they stepped out together for the first time into the direct sunlight. His son's face clouded, even though his eyes were shielded from the light. His wife put her arm around them both.

"He looks like you now," she said, "all that worry and darkness crowded into his few features." He ran his finger over the deep lines in his son's forehead, forcing a smoothness and tranquility that he hoped would settle in both of their souls.

PSALM 145:4-5

One generation shall laud your works
    to another,
    and shall declare your mighty acts.
On the glorious splendor of your
    majesty,
    and on your wondrous works, I
    will meditate.

THE BOOKWORM

At three, he was carefree and inquisitive. He was also demanding, but it was for books. He would take them off the shelves in his bedroom and carry them to his mother or father to read to him. It didn't matter that his mother was fixing supper or his father was painting the front porch. He would go back and forth between them holding up a book, until finally one of them would read to him.

There was little longing in him for what he couldn't have . . . only for what he didn't understand.

PROVERBS 1:8

Hear, my child, your father's
    instruction,
        and do not reject your mother's
            teaching.

Elizabeth the Good

Her friends called her "Elizabeth the Good." Like some medieval lady or abbess, she earned the title because of her unflagging sense of responsibility and kindness.

2 Corinthians 13:5

Examine yourselves to see whether you are living in the faith. Test yourselves. Do you not realize that Jesus Christ is in you?

COMMITMENTS

On the last day he had to be in school, he told his wife, "I'm only going to have two commitments this summer: one to fishing and the other to playing the piano for church."

"But," she said, "what about me?"

"You're not a commitment," he replied. "You're the reason I keep any commitments at all."

EPHESIANS 5:25

Husbands, love your wives, just as Christ loved the church and gave himself up for her.

Coming of Age

His friends refused to laugh when he went into his "old man" routine. They were a little uncomfortable about making fun of what would surely be their fate . . . and a little unsure about how gracefully they would handle it.

Amos 2:14

Flight shall perish from the swift,
   and the strong shall not retain their
   strength.

GOD'S WORK

"I haven't thought about God for so long," he thought, suddenly lost in memories of his Catholic grade school days.

He remembered how the sisters had told him he should be a priest. Imagine him doing God's work!

Then he did something he hadn't done in a long time. He prayed about his own work and remembered that it, too, is God's work.

JOHN 6:29

Jesus answered them, "This is the work of God, that you believe in him whom he has sent."

Life Plan

It was not the job she had pictured for herself when she was in college, but then again she wasn't sure exactly what she should be doing with her life. For the most part she was happy, and she was ready for whatever might happen—good or bad.

Matthew 24:44

"Therefore you also must be ready, for the Son of Man is coming at an unexpected hour."

FOURTH OF JULY

At breakfast his father announced, "We're going to the farm to help your uncle make hay. Now hurry up and get your work shoes on."

The boy hated going to his uncle's farm. He was old enough to help, but his father and uncle never really talked to him. They just told him what to do and told him to do it faster and better.

"It's the Fourth of July," he pouted. "Can't we do something fun?" He hoped his father might remember what it was like to be twelve.

What his father remembered was being twelve during the Great Depression. He wanted his son to learn how to work hard and enjoy the peace of mind that comes from knowing you've done what you could. That was true independence.

JOHN 4:38

"I sent you to reap that for which you did not labor. Others have labored, and you have entered into their labor."

In God's Hands

The old pastor seemed always on the verge of exasperation, and a white handkerchief tucked sloppily in his back pocket was the outward sign of his internal surrender to the providence of God. When he pulled it out to mop his receding brow, it was the sign that he had exhausted his resources. The rest was in God's hands.

Luke 22:42

> "Father, if you are willing, remove
> this cup from me; yet not my will but
> yours be done."

LADY LIBERTY

The neighbors from the cottages around the lake held a parade each year on the Saturday after the Fourth of July. This year the seven-year-old girl was Lady Liberty. Swathed in a sheet, a tinfoil torch held high, she waved to the vacationers who lined the lane. Although she did not know these people, she nodded blessings toward them, filled with a sense that her own good will was as necessary for their happiness as the sun and breeze off the lake.

JEREMIAH 34:15

You yourselves recently repented and did what was right in my sight by proclaiming liberty to one another.

THE FLOWER GARDEN

She carefully tended the small oval of flowers she had set in her front yard. She never cut any blossoms to take into her house. Some inner generosity prompted her to leave them for the people who passed by.

AMOS 9:15

I will plant them upon their land,
   and they shall never again be
      plucked up
   out of the land that I have given them.

THE APARTMENT

It was an old apartment building, built strong and solid by someone who had an eye to the future. Hundreds of tenants would come and go over the years, living lives and leaving memories that only they and the walls would remember.

PSALM 145:4

One generation shall laud your
works to another,
and shall declare your mighty
acts.

FACE-OFF

He told his wife it was their son's tone of voice he couldn't abide.

His wife looked at him with a slight smile. "Dear, he's exactly like you," she said. "If you heard a tone, it's because you put it there. Learn to live with it, or get rid of it in yourself before you try to get rid of it in him."

HOSEA 8:7

For they sow the wind,
and they shall reap the whirlwind.

Macho Man

His wife had taken a sewing job and spent too many late nights trying to get it done. When he came down the basement and put his arm around her, she said: "If we're going to spend time together, you'll have to help me finish this project."

As he sat next to her at the sewing machine, frilly strips of cloth running across his legs, he rationalized this unmanly pursuit. What could be more macho than seducing the woman he loved?

Song of Songs 4:11

Your lips distill nectar, my bride;
    honey and milk are under your
        tongue;
    the scent of your garments is
        like the scent of Lebanon."

Divine Patience

God, you watch what goes wrong in this world,
what gets twisted and torn,
what stutters and creeps,
what winds down into deep, dark places.

We do not understand what holds you back;
why you do not come at us growling mad,
swinging your righteousness like a cleaver
through the tangled mess we make of things.

Hosea 11:4

I led them with cords of human
        kindness,
    with bands of love.
I was to them like those
        who lift infants to their cheeks.
        I bent down to them and fed them.

SPECIAL

In today's educational system, she would be put in a special education class, but there were no such things at that time.

One day during reading, her teacher called on her. The little girl had no clue what was going on. "What are you thinking about?" the teacher asked.

"I was dreaming that you gave me all A's on my report card, and you said I was the smartest girl in class," the girl admitted.

The teacher walked to the child's desk, put her arm around her, and said, "I can't give you all A's on your report card, and I can't tell you that you are the smartest girl in class. However, I can tell you that you are a very nice girl who never hurts anyone—and that makes you special."

PSALM 37:18

The LORD knows the days of the blameless,
    and their heritage will abide forever.

THE CALL

"Two weeks!" she repeated. "It only lasts two weeks, and this retreat will help me understand what God wants of me."

"Are you trying to get away from us?" he asked.

"No," she answered. "I'm trying to get back to you."

ISAIAH 6:8

Then I heard the voice of the Lord saying, "Whom shall I send, and who will go for us?" And I said, "Here am I; send me!"

THE ROBIN

This Saturday morning he came downstairs in a pair of gym shorts. He took a glass of juice out onto the porch and gazed into the bright sunlight of a perfect morning. A robin flew past him and settled in the maple tree he had planted ten years ago.

LUKE 13:18-19

"What is the kingdom of God like? And to what should I compare it? It is like a mustard seed that someone took and sowed in the garden; it grew and became a tree, and the birds of the air made nests in its branches."

An Alien Land

As he walked along the country road that circled the lake, he saw migrant workers in the cucumber fields straightening the vines. He wondered where they came from and how they decided to come to this place.

Genesis 17:8

"And I will give to you, and to your offspring after you, the land where you are now an alien, all the land of Canaan, for a perpetual holding; and I will be their God."

COUSINS

Running around the farmyard with squirt guns in their hands, the three cousins didn't notice their parents were watching, remembering what it was like when they were that young. "Will they always get along this well?" the oldest asked her sister.

"I just hope they realize how much fun they had together, not how far they have drifted apart," the youngest said, with just a touch of regret in her voice.

PROVERBS 17:17

A friend loves at all times,
   and kinsfolk are born to share
      adversity.

The Example

She stood in their bathroom, her hair pulled up loosely on top of her head, her hands on her hips, eyes still puffy from sleep. "I really don't want to wake the kids yet," she said to her husband, who was reading the paper in bed, unshaven and still in his nightshirt.

"It's time to get going," he said, "or we'll never make it to church."

"But the kids will whine and complain the whole time. I don't think I'm up to that this morning," she admitted.

"They whine and complain every Sunday," he pointed out. "It's up to us to set an example for them."

She burst out laughing. "Look at us," she said, "do we look like we could be an example for anyone?"

Luke 12:12
___

"For the Holy Spirit will teach you at that very hour what you ought to say."

The Sign

When he visited his grandmother in the nursing home, she did not recognize him. She was saying her rosary, so he sat beside her quietly until she finished. When she was about to make the sign of the cross at the end, she paused with the rosary cross held in midair. Then she leaned toward him and raised the cross first to his forehead, then to his heart, and then across from one shoulder to the next.

PSALM 16:1-3

Protect me, O God, for in you I take
      refuge.
I say to the LORD, "You are my Lord;
      I have no good apart from you."
As for the holy ones in the land, they are
      the noble,
      in whom is all my delight.

A Place of Her Own

On her twenty-first birthday, her grandfather called her to him and said, "It's time you moved out of your house and went on your own."

"But Grandpa," she said, "I have no money and no place to go. How can I leave home?"

"I have a little money," he said. "I'll send you some every month."

So she moved out the following month. Her parents were sad to see her go, but they knew it was best for their daughter.

Her grandfather lived another ten years. They were good years, she thought to herself as she pulled the weeds from around his headstone.

Exodus 3:17

> "I declare that I will bring you up out of the misery of Egypt, to . . . a land flowing with milk and honey."

GOOD TO BE ALIVE

Sitting on the deck with a glass of lemonade in her hand, watching the July sun set late and low in the west, she let the tensions of the day flow out of her and remembered again how good it was simply to be alive.

ISAIAH 38:16

O Lord, by these things people live,
    and in all these is the life of
      my spirit.
Oh, restore me to health and make
    me live!

SOMEDAY

He thought to himself that someday his wife would
be sorry. Someday she'd wish she treated him
better. He had no specific plan in his head, just
"someday," which—if they both were lucky—
would never come.

MICAH 2:1

Alas for those who devise wickedness
and evil deeds on their beds.

FORGETTING

Their father worked in the mines. He came home coughing and complaining how dark it was inside. Their mother did endless hours of ironing for rich people. This they did to give their children a chance at a better life, never imagining that they would forget where they came from or the God who had gotten them through all the hard times.

ISAIAH 65:9

I will bring forth descendants from Jacob,
    and from Judah inheritors of my
        mountains;
my chosen shall inherit it,
    and my servants shall settle there.

THE CLOWN

"C'mon Daddy," she squealed in anticipation, "show me how you stay underwater so long!"

He hoped she could see through his performance to the really important stuff. There is a trick to staying underwater; there is no trick to loving someone with all your heart and all your soul.

MATTHEW 12:38

> Then some of the scribes and Pharisees said to him, "Teacher, we wish to see a sign from you."

THE WALK

He walked between the rows of cars on the lot. He was not happy about having to buy one. Mostly, he dreaded the hassle. He didn't trust the sales-people. He especially disliked their oily smiles. When he saw a salesperson coming toward him, he turned and walked out without making a decision.

Later he went for a long walk, a kind of test. Could he possibly get along without a car? Could he undergo such a radical conversion in his life?

MICAH 6:8

He has told you, O mortal, what is good;
and what does the LORD require of you
but to do justice, and to love kindness,
and to walk humbly with your God?

CRAVINGS

At the all-night supermarket, he went straight to the salad bar and filled a carton with chopped red onions. His only other purchase was a bottle of mouthwash. The checkout girl said nothing. She had worked late nights long enough to know that some people believed every craving had to be fed.

EXODUS 16:3

> The Israelites said to them, "If only we had died by the hand of the LORD in the land of Egypt, when we sat by the fleshpots and ate our fill of bread; for you have brought us out into this wilderness to kill this whole assembly with hunger."

THE IMITATORS

The school children mocked him, trying on his mannerisms to amuse each other. They didn't realize they were trying on his holiness for size.

JEREMIAH 1:5

Before I formed you in the womb I
    knew you,
      before you were born I consecrated
    you.

Distance

She didn't understand why the Lord sometimes felt so far away, as if there was some great gulf between them. It was not that she was unaware of his presence in those times, only that he seemed to be holding her at arms' length—as if she could only truly listen from a distance.

Matthew 13:1-3

That same day Jesus went out of the house and sat beside the sea. Such great crowds gathered around him that he got into a boat and sat there, while the whole crowd stood on the beach. And he told them many things in parables.

GRANDFATHER'S FARM

The man had hated the farm when he was growing up on it. Now the auctioneer was preparing to sell it off because none of the man's children or grandchildren wanted it. He couldn't force them to value what he himself had grown to love only so reluctantly.

MATTHEW 13:3-4

"Listen! A sower went out to sow.
And as he sowed, some seeds fell on
the path, and the birds came and ate
them up."

Scorched Earth

She had boundless enthusiasm and fell in love easily, but her passing fancies could never match the energy required to keep them. A friend told her that she left a path of scorched earth behind her.

Matthew 13:5-6

"Other seeds fell on rocky ground, where they did not have much soil, and they sprang up quickly, since they had no depth of soil. But when the sun rose, they were scorched; and since they had no roots, they withered away."

A Moment Lost

This was the real vacation time for him—walking alone in the woods, the lake waters lapping gently off in the distance, the sun burning itself off the horizon. The sense of peace was so near that he felt he could actually reach out and touch God.

At dinner that evening, he tried to hold onto the peace he had found in the woods. But everyone was talking and drinking too much—and the moment was gone.

MATTHEW 13:7

"Other seeds fell among the thorns, and the thorns grew up and choked them."

Success

In the end it may simply be what we have done with what God gave us in the first place that determines the success of our lives. Which is why gratitude is more important than supplication.

Matthew 13:8

"Other seeds fell on good soil and brought forth grain, some a hundred-fold, some sixty, some thirty. Let anyone with ears listen!"

THE FONT

The holy water font hanging by her parents' back door has been dried up for years. But her mother still dips her fingers into the calcified bottom as she leaves to go grocery shopping or to get her hair fixed.

EXODUS 40:36

Whenever the cloud was taken up from
the tabernacle, the Israelites would set
out on each stage of their journey.

REFRIGERATOR ART

Like so many other refrigerators in America, theirs was adorned with colored drawings and starred papers—a visual barrage of offerings held up for their approval and praise, waved before them in delight and accomplishment.

LEVITICUS **23:10**

When you enter the land that I am giving you and you reap its harvest, you shall bring the sheaf of the first fruits of your harvest to the priest.

RIGHT RELATIONSHIP

To stand in fear of God is to stand in right relationship with others, treating them with respect, honesty, and justice.

LEVITICUS 25:17

You shall not cheat one another, but you shall fear your God; for I am the LORD your God.

OUR FATHER

Her favorite part of Mass was when they all held hands for the Our Father. She always sat by her daddy because his big hand in hers made her feel safe and loved.

LUKE 11:1-2

One of his disciples said to him, "Lord, teach us to pray, as John taught his disciples." He said to them, "When you pray, say:
"Father, hallowed be your name. Your kingdom come."

PEACE

He was old enough to know that he didn't have to return violence for violence. But apparently he was not old enough to make peace.

JEREMIAH 28:9

"As for the prophet who prophesies peace, when the word of that prophet comes true, then it will be known that the LORD has truly sent the prophet."

Memoirs

When she turned fifty, she decided to write her memoirs. After a month, she had written one page of introductory prose—and there she got stuck. She had said everything there was to say, for she had never risked much, never sacrificed much, never loved much.

JOHN 15:13

"No one has greater love than this, to
lay down one's life for one's friends."

THE BROTHERS

They stood at the side of the bed, each suffering his own pain at the sure death of their father, yet they did not speak to one another. After twenty years of silent anger, they had forgotten how.

MATTHEW 5:22

"But I say to you that if you are angry with a brother or sister, you will be liable to judgment; and if you insult a brother or sister, you will be liable to the council; and if you say, 'You fool,' you will be liable to the hell of fire."

Rain Dance

On his ninetieth birthday, he promised if it rained he would go out in the street and dance in it. He was, of course, too frail to dance by himself, but she would help him. Long ago she learned to be grateful for miracles, whether they happened in body or spirit or nature.

Numbers 20:10

Moses and Aaron gathered the assembly together before the rock, and he said to them, "Listen, you rebels, shall we bring water for you out of this rock?"

GRAND CANYON

On the way up and out of the Grand Canyon, his heart began to pound and his head went dizzy. When they finally made the crest, the sun was setting as they looked across the incredible landscape. His daughter put her arm around him and said: "I'm proud of you, Dad."

As touching as that scene was, however, the father was thinking more about God and the brevity—and wonder—of life.

DEUTERONOMY 4:35

To you it was shown so that you would acknowledge that the LORD is God; there is no other besides him.

Baked Bean Communion

For thirty years, their family reunion had been held on the second Saturday of August. The matriarch of the family, the last to remember the old country, died last year. Two of her grandsons had volunteered to make her baked beans. They held the first spoonful up to the lips of the youngest among them, her first solid food.

Deuteronomy 6:11-12

And when you have eaten your fill, take care that you do not forget the Lord, who brought you out of the land of Egypt.

BEFORE THE FALL

When we root out the less noble parts of us, it creates a vacuum that draws us all the way back to Eden . . . before the fall.

EPHESIANS 4:31

Put away from you all bitterness
and wrath and anger and wran-
gling and slander, together with
all malice.

Reconstruction

He surveyed the slum that was soon to be torn
down. How much easier it was to equate God's
creation with those places humanity has never
touched than with the squalor that humanity has
wrought. This thought made it easier, of course,
for him to dismiss the lives of those who lived in
the buildings about to be torn down.

Genesis 1:26

Then God said, "Let us make humankind
in our image, according to our likeness."

"UNTIL DEATH DO US PART"

She smiled when her husband-to-be forgot to repeat the marriage promises after the priest. Like her, he was lost in a moment they both knew they could never sustain. Good and bad times would startle them into the present. Sickness and health would alternately accompany them into the future.

DEUTERONOMY 31:8

It is the LORD who goes before you.
He will be with you; he will not fail
you or forsake you. Do not fear or
be dismayed.

STILL GOING STRONG

Getting old bugged him. It wasn't that his eyesight
was so bad or that he was all that weak; it was
just that no one wanted to follow his lead anymore—even in bridge!

DEUTERONOMY 34:7

> Moses was one hundred twenty years
> old when he died; his sight was
> unimpaired and his vigor had not
> abated.

TRUTH

Those who bring the truth to life always give up
something of themselves.

2 CORINTHIANS 2:17

For we are not peddlers of God's
word like so many; but in Christ
we speak as persons of sincerity,
as persons sent from God and
standing in his presence.

Pure Love

The fact that we know many kinds of love—from parental care to adolescent infatuation to sustaining friendship to spousal commitment—suggests that we are capable of loving God in a unique way that neither destroys our freedom nor exhausts our capacity to love our neighbor as ourselves.

Ezekiel 16:8

I pledged myself to you and entered into a covenant with you, says the Lord God, and you became mine.

The Project

When they were putting the finishing touches on a major project, the boss paused and said, "I really appreciate the way you all pulled together as a team to get this done."

After three years of working together, the five of them had learned to discipline their tongues and forgive each other almost anything.

Hebrews 12:3

Consider him who endured such hostility against himself from sinners, so that you may not grow weary or lose heart.

THE INHERITANCE

At seventeen, he prayed not to inherit his mother's temper. He spent years practicing compliance, pouring all his passion into this art. Now his daughter prays not to inherit her father's passivity.

EZEKIEL 18:4

Know that all lives are mine; the life of the parent as well as the life of the child is mine.

POSSESSIONS

The young man in the gospel couldn't deal with
the answer Jesus gave him, and "he went away
grieving, for he had many possessions." An older
man may have already seen some of these
possessions turn to dust and would have been in
a better position to understand the Teacher.

MATTHEW 19:21

Jesus said to him, "If you wish to be
perfect, go, sell your possessions, and
give the money to the poor, and you
will have treasure in heaven; then
come, follow me."

Bad Day

She had had a really bad day. Nothing had gone right. Finally, when her grilled cheese sandwich burned black, she looked up to heaven and said calmly, "Lord if it weren't for the fact that I still have a roof over my head and some leftover tuna in the fridge, I'd begin to wonder if you even exist."

Judges 6:13

The angel of the LORD appeared to him and said to him, "The LORD is with you, you mighty warrior." Gideon answered him, "But sir, if the LORD is with us, why then has all this happened to us?"

Manna from Heaven

Most days she sits alone in her one-room apartment and listens to the radio. If you ask her, she
will tell you she has no friends. Strangers put food
outside her door. Her landlady sneaks in and
leaves new clothes . . . and occasionally disinfects
the place. She accepts all these things as manna
from heaven—which may not be far from the truth.

Ezekiel 34:11

For thus says the Lord God: I myself will
search for my sheep, and will seek them out.

Clown Ministry

He liked to paint his face, put on his clown outfit, and go downtown on a busy Saturday. He would hand out roses to the women and suckers to the children, telling them simply, "God loves you." Many people thought him foolish; some looked for a donation basket and were surprised when they could find none.

Psalm 40:10

I have not hidden your saving help
    within my heart,
  I have spoken of your faithfulness
    and your salvation;
I have not concealed your steadfast
    love and your faithfulness
  from the great congregation.

No Regrets

On their fiftieth wedding anniversary, her husband asked her if she had any regrets. "It hasn't always been easy," she admitted, "but when I married you I promised to be faithful to you in every way, and I asked God to help me keep that promise. I would have more regrets if I had not kept my word."

RUTH 1:16

"Where you go, I will go;
    where you lodge, I will lodge;
your people shall be my people,
    and your God my God."

FOOTPRINTS

He raced to get to his own secret stretch of beach.
He liked to believe that only he and God knew
about this place. Parting the last bit of underbrush,
he breathed a sigh of relief. As usual, the beach
was deserted. As he walked to the water, he
noticed the footprints. He thought they could only
have been made by God. He fit his own feet into
them and took giant steps across the sand.

EZEKIEL 43:7

> He said to me: Mortal, this is the
> place of my throne and the place for
> the soles of my feet, where I will
> reside among the people of Israel
> forever.

THE CAREGIVER

She had cared for her sick mother for over ten years. It had become a daily grind: call her mom before work, see her right after work; spend all day Saturday shopping for her, cleaning her apartment, getting her prescriptions; pick her up for Sunday church and Sunday dinner, take her home, talk to her, write letters for her. Some nights she prayed God to take her mother soon, not for her mother's sake but for her own.

ROMANS 8:26

Likewise the Spirit helps us in our weakness; for we do not know how to pray as we ought, but that very Spirit intercedes with sighs too deep for words.

New Baby Brother

The boy eyed his new little brother with suspicion. He poked him softly on the arm. His brother didn't seem to notice. Harder, a second time. Still no reaction. Finally, a third time, hard into the pink flesh he pressed. His brother cried, eyes unable to focus on the source of the pain.

His parents had watched all this patiently. He looked horrified and turned to them. "The new baby hurts."

"Yes," said his mother. "And it's your special job to make sure he never hurts again."

2 Corinthians 9:1-2

> Now it is not necessary for me to write you about the ministry to the saints, for I know your eagerness, which is the subject of my boasting about you.

CAREER CHANGE

On the day he went in to tell them he was quitting, he had no firm plan in mind. He just knew he had to find a job where he could make a difference in people's lives. All he had was the hope that he was making the right move, that the right job would come along.

He was surprised when his team leader looked at him and said, "Thanks for all your good work here. I know you made a difference in a lot of people's lives."

2 THESSALONIANS 2:16

Now may our Lord Jesus Christ himself and God our Father, who loved us and through grace gave us eternal comfort and good hope, comfort your hearts and strengthen them in every good work and word.

ALL HER CHILDREN

She had had an abortion when she was seventeen. She had not told her parents or her best friend or even the father—a careless eighteen-year-old.

When she became pregnant again at twenty-one, with another year of college to go, she could not bring herself to have another abortion. She carried this child to term and gave him up for adoption.

Now, at age thirty-two, holding her new baby against her breast, her husband asleep in the chair by her bed, she wept.

JEREMIAH 31:15-16

> Rachel is weeping for her children;
>   she refuses to be comforted for
>   her children,
>   because they are no more.
> Thus says the LORD:
> Keep your voice from weeping,
>   and your eyes from tears;
> for there is a reward for your work.

WORRIES

Rocking in the chair her children gave her for her seventy-fifth birthday, she could no longer remember the details of any of the things that had worried her for all these years. And she realized that her worrying had never changed a thing nor brought her a surplus of mercy for the future.

PSALM 90:4

For a thousand years in your sight
   are like yesterday when it is past,
   or like a watch in the night.

THE LABORER

Coming home to his two-room shack each night, dirty and exhausted, he had to keep reminding himself that God never promised him wealth, only that there would be a place waiting for him at the eternal banquet. There, seated with saints and sinners alike, washed clean by the blood of the lamb, his dirty fingernails would not be an embarrassment.

PSALM 90:17

Let the favor of the Lord our
God be upon us,
and prosper for us the work of
our hands—
O prosper the work of our hands!

ENCOURAGEMENT

In the beginning she was hesitant to make any suggestions to her supervisor. After they became friends, he encouraged her to think on her own and she gained enough confidence to tell him when she thought he was making a mistake and what he could do to increase production.

Today he told her the company was moving him and he had recommended her for his job. When she protested, he told her in a tone that was both confident and prodding, "Don't worry. You'll be better at it than I ever was."

1 THESSALONIANS 4:1

We ask and urge you in the Lord
Jesus that, as you learned from us
how you ought to live and to please
God (as, in fact, you are doing), you
should do so more and more.

GOD TALK

Three children play in the church nursery while their parents are at Mass. Tired of playing with blocks and dolls, they speak softly to one another.

The youngest puts a question to the other two, "Why do Mommy and Daddy bring us here?"

The oldest, feeling responsible to come up with an answer, responds, "Because when they were young, their parents brought them here."

The middle child, face pressed against the stained glass in an attempt to see inside, says, "But why did Grandma and Grandpa bring Mom and Dad here?"

The oldest replies, "Because someone brought them."

The youngest child says, "I betcha it was God."

1 CORINTHIANS 2:4-5

My speech and my proclamation were not with plausible words of wisdom, but with a demonstration of the Spirit and of power, so that your faith might rest not on human wisdom but on the power of God.

THE READER

Pressed for a reader at the last moment, the priest asked the young woman if she would do it for him. "Do you think you can pronounce all the words?" he asked.

She looked at him with the scorn of an eighteen-year-old. "Of course I can pronounce all the words. I'm a lifelong Catholic," she exclaimed.

But the reading did not go well. Embarrassed and humbled, she said to the priest after Mass, "Guess I shouldn't have been so confident."

"Oh, confidence is great, as long as it's combined with humility," he said.

LUKE 4:16

When he came to Nazareth, where he had been brought up, he went to the synagogue on the sabbath day, as was his custom. He stood up to read.

FIRST DAY OF SCHOOL

She walked him to the end of the driveway on his first day of kindergarten. When the bus arrived he got on, lifting his leg high to reach the first step made for big people. He did not look back.

When he came home she was there, waiting for him at the end of the driveway. He was a mess. Torn shirt, bloody nose, tattered papers containing his first day's work in school. Her heart went out to him.

The next day she walked him to the end of the driveway again. Before the bus came, he stooped down to pick up a few stones and put them in his pocket. For the first time it occurred to her that he might be the aggressor and not the aggrieved.

1 CORINTHIANS 3:3

> For as long as there is jealousy and quarreling among you, are you not of the flesh, and behaving according to human inclinations?

Cured but Not Healed

People pray to be cured when they are sick. But when they are well, some forget the prayer of thanksgiving and get on with their lives. All healing requires a response.

Then he stood over her and rebuked the fever, and it left her. Immediately she got up and began to serve them.

CHARM SCHOOL

When she was in sixth grade her mother sent her to charm school, hoping it would give her enough grace to divert her tomboy tendencies. On graduation day, she walked erect and confident, head up, back straight.

Twenty-five years later, as she walked to the grave of her ten-year-old son, she let her body slump against her husband. Grace comes not from walking with your head up but from walking in the love of God.

COLOSSIANS 1:11-12

> May you be made strong with all the strength that comes from his glorious power, and may you be prepared to endure everything with patience, while joyfully giving thanks to the Father, who has enabled you to share in the inheritance of the saints in the light.

THE JUGGLER

Her grandparents were over and her twin sister was in another room. She picked up three apples, polished them on her sweatshirt, and began to juggle them. Her grandparents applauded and she glowed.

Her grandmother placed her arm around her and said, "How clever you are."

The child corrected her. "My sister is clever," she said. "I'm well coordinated."

1 CORINTHIANS 3:18

Do not deceive yourselves. If you think that you are wise in this age, you should become fools so that you may become wise.

THE MAGIC MIRROR

What made him so irresistible to others was his
ability to look honestly at himself and admit his
faults. He didn't have the conceit to think that only
others could be fallible. Whatever he saw in them
he could always find in himself.

PSALM 24:3-4

Who shall ascend the hill of the LORD?
    And who shall stand in his holy place?
Those who have clean hands and pure hearts,
    who do not lift up their souls to what is false.

BEST FRIEND

She was always doing little things that others hardly noticed, and that made her the best friend anyone ever had.

2 CORINTHIANS 4:6

For it is the God who said, "Let light shine out of darkness," who has shone in our hearts to give the light of the knowledge of the glory of God in the face of Jesus Christ.

TREADING WATER

His daughter brought home the "man of her dreams" when she was seventeen. A thin, sullen boy who never looked him in the eye, never said much, and never showed affection for his daughter. "He makes me feel like a million bucks," she said.

The four of them sat at table at an all-you-can-eat buffet restaurant as his daughter announced her intention to marry the young man. After dinner, the young man feigned payment by reaching for his wallet, but the father put up his hand, pulled out his wallet, and counted out just the right amount. Then he tucked a five dollar tip under his plate.

Halfway to the cashier stand, the young man said he'd forgotten something. Back at the table, he quickly reached under the plate, picked up the tip money, and put it in his pocket. The father caught the maneuver out of the corner of his eye and felt a wave of sorrow that he was not sure he could tread.

ECCLESIASTES 1:15

> What is crooked cannot be made straight,
> and what is lacking cannot be counted.

Parenting Wisdom

It was an odd bit of advice he picked up some-where: Never say "No" when your children first ask you to do something. Tell them you'll think about it. The delay has two possible effects. Your children may become distracted by some other passing fancy—or they may try to bribe you with loving deeds.

He wondered if God responds similarly.

Colossians 1:23

Continue securely established and steadfast in the faith, without shifting from the hope promised by the gospel that you have heard, which has been proclaimed to every crea-ture under heaven.

Sunday Stroll

Each Sunday he would pile his wife and children in the car and drive them to a piece of land not far from where he grew up. Together, they would walk through the woods, admiring tall trees and noting the tiny seedlings that would never grow because of the shade. His children would run ahead, grabbing sticks and flinging them at each other or at birds in the brush.

The walk lasted just long enough to remind him of where he came from and of how good it is to be alive.

Isaiah 55:12

For you shall go out in joy,
    and be led back in peace;
the mountains and the hills before you
      shall burst into song,
    and all the trees of the field shall
      clap their hands.

Denial

There were little bits of self-denial he had picked up through the years: no more than one cookie at a time, only one pat of butter no matter how large the roll, no meat on Fridays, only one glass of wine with dinner, no sweets after lunch, and no snacking during the week.

These deprivations had been drummed into him by his mother. It occurred to him that, not only had they stuck with him, but they all had to do with food. As he grew older, he did not see how these things could do God any good, but he did know that they helped keep his cholesterol low.

Romans 8:28

We know that all things work together for good for those who love God, who are called according to his purpose.

Friday the Thirteenth

He asked the cashier the date as he began to write out his check. "The thirteenth" she said, "Friday the thirteenth."

He wished she hadn't reminded him. Bad things were supposed to happen on Friday the thirteenth. Now he would spend the rest of the day waiting for some bad luck to occur instead of being on the lookout for signs of God's grace.

Colossians 2:8

> See to it that no one takes you captive through philosophy and empty deceit, according to human tradition, according to the elemental spirits of the universe, and not according to Christ.

EPIDEMIC

At first, the class was impressed by the newest member's stories of his deeds of courage and derring-do. In a few weeks, they no longer believed the boy's stories. Instead, they were all trying to outdo each other in tales of bravado.

1 CORINTHIANS 5:6

Your boasting is not a good thing. Do you not know that a little yeast leavens the whole batch of dough?

Captain Courageous

He is in sixth grade and captain of the school safety patrol. He takes his job seriously, keeping an eye out for younger children crossing the street and reporting cars that drive too fast through the crossing zones.

Responsibility has been good for him, but someday he will learn that no matter how careful he is there will always be some sadness he will not be able to control.

Luke 12:25-26

And can any of you by worrying add a single hour to your span of life? If then you are not able to do so small a thing as that, why do you worry about the rest?

DETOURS

She had tried them all—the cults, the gurus, the new wave spiritualists, even a "religion" that claimed it didn't matter what you believed. Finally, she returned to her childhood faith, for she always knew, in her heart of hearts, that she would never touch God's hand through pathways created purely by human hands.

MATTHEW 24:24-26

"False messiahs and false prophets will appear and produce great signs and omens, to lead astray. Take note, I have told you beforehand. So, if they say to you, 'Look! He is in the wilderness,' do not go out. If they say, 'Look! He is in the inner rooms,' do not believe it."

THE OTHER CHEEK

The lawyer could never understand how someone
could turn the other cheek. Oh, he knew how you
could forgive someone you loved a lot, after a
while. But to let a stranger defeat you in court...no,
this had nothing to do with his being a Christian.

1 CORINTHIANS 6:7

In fact, to have lawsuits at all with
one another is already a defeat for
you.

THE EMPTY FIELD

She walked out to the edge of her driveway and looked into the park across the street. In the midst of this teeming city, she was grateful for one small place where she could see only what God had planted.

LUKE 6:12

Now during those days he went out to the mountain to pray; and he spent the night in prayer to God.

THE ROCK

He always liked the idea of Jesus changing Simon's name to Peter—"Rock." He wondered if the Lord had a nickname for him too...and what it might be.

ISAIAH 43:1

Do not fear, for I have redeemed you;
I have called you by name, you are mine.

FALSE PIETY

He carefully made the sign of the cross and knelt with perfect posture while the rest of the assembly shuffled noisily waiting for Mass to begin. He stood for the opening prayer and sat as the lector proclaimed the first reading. His mind wandered to tomorrow morning's schedule and a luncheon meeting with his stockbroker. When the collection basket was handed to him, he took out a single dollar bill. Noticing how worn and faded it was reminded him of the lawn chair cushions he had stored at the cottage earlier that day. He made a mental note to replace them next spring.

ISAIAH 29:13

Because these people draw near with
    their mouths
    and honor me with their lips,
    while their hearts are far from me,
and their worship of me is a human
        commandment learned by rote;
so I will again do
    amazing things with this people,
    shocking and amazing.

Falling Leaves

Each year when he saw the first leaf fall, he got a little scared. Maybe it was true, what Saint Paul and the Lord said: this world is passing away.

Hebrews 13:14

For here we have no lasting city, but
we are looking for the city that is to
come.

WHY LOVE?

He put his arm around his maternal grandmother and said, "You're my favorite grandmother." He did it within sight and hearing of his paternal grandmother, a woman who spent a great deal of time criticizing the boy's clothes and manners.

His father pulled him aside and suggested this was not very polite. "I wasn't trying to be polite," he told his dad with straightforward innocence. "I was trying to get Grandma to lay off me for a while."

His father put his arm around him and said, "She's my mother and I love her. You can love her, too, if you work at it."

"Why do I have to love her?" his son said.

His father told him, "In this world we are commanded to love. Sometimes it is easy, sometimes not. In the next world, we won't need a commandment to love. It will be automatic."

COLOSSIANS 3:14

Above all, clothe yourselves with
love, which binds everything together
in perfect harmony.

CHOCOLATE

She always loved chocolate. Her favorite birthday cake was the made-from-scratch flat-pan chocolate cake her mother baked.

Her husband also loved chocolate, but he was allergic to it. He always told her it was okay if she wanted to make it for herself, but she knew that was hard on him. So, after forty years of marriage, she hardly remembers what chocolate tastes like.

1 CORINTHIANS 8:13

> Therefore, if food is a cause of their falling, I will never eat meat, so that I may not cause one of them to fall.

Neurotic

She readily admits she is neurotic. Long ago, she came to terms with this part of herself. If the Lord will take her into heaven this way, she will live with herself on earth this way.

PSALM 139:1-3

O Lord, you have searched me and
known me.
You know when I sit down and when I
rise up;
you discern my thoughts from far
away.
You search out my path and my lying
down,
and are acquainted with all my ways.

REMEMBER ME?

He noticed that his brother went to church regularly and seemed to be getting more involved in his parish. He was tempted to write the whole thing off as a decent guy gone soft on religion. But his brother never even brought up the subject—not over dinner, not when they were out shooting hoops, not even when their mother died.

One day, the man found himself praying for the first time in a long time. "God, remember me? We used to know each other pretty well. What does my brother know that I don't?"

PSALM 139:23-24

Search me, O God, and know my heart;
    test me and know my thoughts.
See if there is any wicked way in me,
    and lead me in the way everlasting.

THE COMMISSION

At dinner on the day Joseph Cardinal Bernardin was buried, the priest said sadly, "The cardinal was a good man."

Another priest at the table pointed a finger at him and said, "Bernardin didn't tell it like it was. He never preached the real gospel of sin and repentance."

At that moment, the first priest wished that he knew the number of times the word "sin" is used in the gospels versus the number of times "love" is used.

PROVERBS 10:12

Hatred stirs up strife,
But love covers all offenses.

BABY OF THE FAMILY

The youngest of eight children, he was born late in his parent's lives, twelve years after his next oldest brother. His parents doted on him, gave him everything. His mother sent him to bed with milk shakes. His father bought him bags full of tiny candy bars. They slipped him dollar bills when they went into town so he could buy other treats. He had the bedroom next to theirs on the first floor.

When the boy grew up, he could never get himself together. He couldn't explain it to his children or to his wife. He simply left them, not unhappily or with acrimony, but with a kind of nonchalance that bewildered him as much as them. He found a one-bedroom house and took a salesman's job traveling the country. Last Halloween, while shopping in a grocery store, he noticed bags of tiny candy bars. He bought four bags and mailed one to each of his three children and one to his wife.

1 TIMOTHY 1:15

> The saying is sure and worthy of full acceptance, that Christ Jesus came into the world to save sinners—of whom I am the foremost.

Religious Ed

She sits on the floor waiting for her young students to arrive. It's Wednesday night and she's already had a long day teaching second graders the fundamentals of reading and writing. Now she is going to teach another group about their religion.

As the children come in, she greets them warmly, asking about their day and helping them with their coats. When everyone has arrived, she lights a candle and one student turns out the lights. She watches as each one makes the sign of the cross, correcting those who start with the wrong hand. Then they pray. Odd, she thinks, that these young minds carry burdens. They pray for big things: for children who have no food, for people who have no homes, for peace though they've never known war, and for the child in the newspaper whose "brain 'sploded."

The teacher is sure that if they can pray like this they already know a lot about God.

Luke 6:40

"A disciple is not above the teacher,
but everyone who is fully qualified
will be like the teacher."

STONE IDOLS

When she saw the life-size Buddha in the store window she wanted it immediately. It would go with her elephant coffee tables, cement rabbits, knight in armor, and cigar store Indian that crowd the rooms of her small house.

Her seventeen-year-old daughter put her foot down. "You can't keep buying this stuff, Mom. What's going to happen when you die? None of us will want this junk."

Her mother sighed and thought to herself that these stone and wood and plaster images were much less trouble than her flesh-and-blood family.

1 CORINTHIANS 10:14

Therefore, my dear friends, flee from the worship of idols. I speak as to sensible people; judge for yourselves what I say.

Autumn Lovers

Walking through the first of autumn's fallen leaves, they were young again. Some who saw them thought they looked a little silly, these old people holding hands, kicking up leaves, and speaking in low tones to each other. Others were jealous that they didn't have the time to do the same thing with someone they loved.

Psalm 125:1

Those who trust in the Lord are like
   Mount Zion,
      which cannot be moved, but
      abides forever.

CHECKOUT

"It's time to pay now," the clerk said.

"Oh dear. I'm afraid I'm not doing this right," the elderly lady said confusedly. "I've never had to bag the groceries myself."

"I'll help you after you finish paying," the clerk assured her.

But the clerk did not help her. Instead, she began checking out the next customer, who bagged his own groceries and pushed himself past the elderly lady still struggling with the task. Maybe he would have helped her, but he was already late for church.

JAMES 1:22-24

> But be doers of the word, and not
> merely hearers who deceive them-
> selves. For if any are hearers of the
> word and not doers, they are like
> those who look at themselves in a
> mirror; for they look at themselves
> and, on going away, immediately
> forget what they were like.

ANGELS REVISITED

She slips into the pew and prays silently for her daughter, who will deliver her first child any day now. She is startled when the priest begins talking about how a past generation made room at their second-grade desks for their angels.

"You have a guardian angel," the priest says. "That's what we were taught and that's why we made room for them. But we grew cynical and left our angels behind us, along with our crayons and our innocence. But to teach a child, or even an adult, that we are never far from God's presence was both a good and true thing."

It occurred to her that her daughter should know that as the days shortened before the birth of her child God remained close by. She tried to remember the prayer: "Angel of God, my guardian dear, to whom God's love commits me here . . . ."

PSALM 91:11-12

For he will command his angels
    concerning you
  to guard you in all your ways.
On their hands they will bear you up,
    so that you will not dash your
      foot against a stone.

VISITATION

It is a Sunday night scene repeated across the United States. A car pulls up to a curb. Inside there are hushed tones, gentle conversation, and kisses good-bye. Seat belts unbuckle, the man walks around the car to open the passenger door. Then he goes to the trunk and pulls out a canvas overnight bag, a pillow, and a teddy bear. He walks his child to her mother's door, where he watches as the little girl is welcomed and em-braced. As his daughter slips inside, he hands her mother the bag. The parents' eyes meet in a subdued greeting. Information is exchanged that once was shared at the breakfast table.

MATTHEW 19:4-5

He answered, "Have you not read that the one who made them at the beginning 'made them male and female,' and said, 'For this reason a man shall leave his father and mother and be joined to his wife, and the two shall become one flesh'?"

"Pass" the Bread

Two young men, friends since childhood, meet after months of separation. Effortlessly, they take up where they left off. A loaf of homemade bread, a generous impulse for the unexpected dinner invitation, becomes an imagined football. It sails in the air passing through stubborn branches of the backyard oak tree and is caught in the open arms of the receiver. The bread is ruined as food but has served a nourishing purpose for their souls.

Luke 11:3

"Give us each day our daily bread."

THE PEOPLE-PLEASER

He claims to be a people-pleaser. He is always adjusting his personality to suit the people he's with. His own identity lies somewhere beneath the clown, the boisterous joker, the boy scout, the favorite grandchild, the trashy buddy, and the dull accountant.

"It's just a matter of giving people what they want," he says in a candid moment. "There's no pressure to be 'me,' only the challenge of figuring out what somebody wants me to be."

"But do you know who you are?"

"Like Jesus, I'm all things to all people." He smiles and extends his hand in something too close to a blessing to go unnoticed and too discrete to be a joke. He catches the eye of an acquaintance, who reaches out a hand to greet him—and the boundary between what is and what could be blurs again.

2 CORINTHIANS 13:5

> Examine yourselves to see whether
> you are living in the faith. Test
> yourselves. Do you not realize that
> Jesus Christ is in you?

HIV-Positive

He doesn't know how to say it and so he just blurts it out: "I was working with a patient who was HIV-positive and I pricked myself with the needle I had just used to draw his blood."

The statement hangs in the air, which has suddenly gotten thicker and less predictable as a guarantor of life. His friend says nothing. There has to be more to a story that threatens the life of someone you care about.

Job 9:27-28

If I say, 'I will forget my complaint;
  I will put off my sad countenance
    and be of good cheer,'
I become afraid of all my suffering,
  for I know you will not hold me
    innocent.

Autumn Bride

"I want to marry you when the leaves are golden and the grass still green," he had said. So an October wedding was planned.

As she walked into church, a single leaf floated and caught in her veil. A bridesmaid went to remove it but she stayed her hand. "Leave it," she said. "Even when things seem to be dying, there is hope."

Romans 8:24-25

> For in hope we were saved. Now
> hope that is seen is not hope. For who
> hopes for what is seen? But if we
> hope for what we do not see, we wait
> for it with patience.

FALSE PREGNANCY

He married at thirty-five in a town where girls were pregnant at sixteen, worn out and tired by the time they were thirty, and surprisingly formidable when they hit forty. His wife doted on him in the way the hopeful treasure rabbit's feet and four-leaf clovers.

At forty-four, no one expected her to get pregnant. He sat on a stool in Fat's Tap, bought a round of beer for everyone, and announced, "The Mrs. is pregnant. Drink up boys."

His wife kept getting bigger and bigger, but there was no baby—only the weight brought on by their frustrated dreams.

ROMANS 8:22-23

We know that the whole creation
has been groaning in labor pains
until now; and not only the creation, but we ourselves, who have
the first fruits of the Spirit, groan
inwardly while we wait for adoption, the redemption of our bodies.

THE HOLD-OUT

His restaurant had never done much local business. Most of his trade came from travelers on the state highway that passed ten feet from his parking lot. When the highway department drew up plans for a new four-lane road slated to go right through his restaurant, he figured he'd hit the jackpot.

The state offered him a fair price and increased it twice when he refused to sell. He had decided to settle on the next offer when the highway department went back to the drawing board. They added a little jog around his property...with no immediate access to the restaurant.

PROVERBS 15:27

Those who are greedy for unjust gain
     make trouble for their households,
but those who hate bribes will live.

THE REBEL

She sat sullen and defiant in the corner of the classroom as the young priest tried to talk about faith. "Why do you believe in God?" he asked them.

She was the only one to raise her hand. "I don't," she said.

"Of course you do," he said, smiling encouragingly.

"No, I don't," she said clearly.

"Then why are you here?" he asked

"If I could answer that," she said, "I might be able to believe in God."

JOB 3:23

"Why is light given to one who
cannot see the way,
whom God has fenced in?"

ONE DAY AT A TIME

She worried a lot about her father. Today, when he returned from the doctor, he called her and said: "It's not good. The doctor said there was no more he could do for me."

"What does that mean?" she said.

"It means I have to live one day at a time. Of course, that's the way we all should be living, anyway."

PSALM 27:13-14

> I believe that I shall see the goodness
>   of the LORD
>   in the land of the living.
> Wait for the LORD;
>   be strong, and let your heart take
>   courage;
>   wait for the LORD!

THE DATE

After the Fall Festival dance, four of them met at his house. His parents weren't home and he had the house to himself. He was feeling mighty proud, for he had snagged the most popular girl in the class as his date. He found the key to his parents' liquor cabinet and started to pour some drinks. Abruptly, his date stood up.

"I don't need this," she said, heading for the door.

There was an uncomfortable silence as she walked out. Finally, the other couple followed. He stood alone, contemplating the four filled glasses of booze and wondering why his friends had left.

"Jerks," he muttered under his breath. He picked up a glass, sat down, grabbed the remote, and switched on the TV set.

ZECHARIAH 8:23

"Let us go with you, for we have heard that God is with you."

THE GIFT

He was only five when his parents announced they were adopting a sister for him. He was not pleased. He was old enough to know this would change things. He had learned about "sharing" in preschool and day care and it was not something at which he excelled. On the day his parents brought his new sister home, he played with her patiently and even "shared." As they were putting the two of them down for a nap, he announced: "We can keep her until supper and then you have to take her back."

"Take her back where?" his father asked.

"Take her back to God," he said, remembering what he'd learned about where babies came from.

"But God gave her to us," his mother said.

"God should ask first. And God should say `please,'" he said, proud of himself for that rebuttal. He would learn, many years later, that God always gives but God never asks.

JAMES 1:17

> Every generous act of giving, with every perfect gift, is from above, coming down from the Father of lights, with whom there is no variation or shadow due to change.

THE SPIDER'S WEB

A spider's web stretched across the screen, which was now closed against an October draft. Bunched and milky looking, it would catch no more insects, provide no more food for the spider who had long ago crawled away to spin other webs on other screens.

ECCLESIASTES 3:22

There is nothing better than that all should enjoy their work, for that is their lot; who can bring them to see what will be after them?

Pumpkins

It has been a bad year for pumpkins. Last year, every pumpkin was plump and round and perfectly orange. This year, spring was long and cold, blocking out the sun with dark and heavy clouds. The delayed growing season means that what few pumpkins can be found are thin and green and small.

Still, Halloween is just around the corner.

Genesis 8:22

> As long as the earth endures,
>> seedtime and harvest, cold and
>>> heat,
> summer and winter, day and night,
>> shall not cease.

RETIREMENT PLAN

When he retired, his wife made a rule: he had to be out of the house by ten every morning and couldn't return until lunch time. She didn't care where he went or what he did. His friends thought this was a silly rule, but he knew better. He found a part-time job, which gave him just enough time away from the house to allow him to greet her with a kiss when he returned and to tell her about his day.

LUKE 10:38-39

Now as they went on their way, he entered a certain village, where a woman named Martha welcomed him into her home. She had a sister named Mary, who sat at the Lord's feet and listened to what he was saying.

Shadow on the Wall

The old crucifix had hung in her bedroom since she first moved into the little house her son had built for her. One day while dusting, she dropped it and it shattered. She did not buy a new one. The faded wallpaper had a clear, clean imprint of the cross where it had hung so long on her wall.

John 19:31

Since it was the day of Preparation, the Jews did not want the bodies left on the cross during the sabbath, especially because that sabbath was a day of great solemnity. So they asked Pilate to have the legs of the crucified men broken and the bodies removed.

THE CONFLICT

He knew about the rice paddies and the swelter-
ing heat only from the few things his parents had
told him, and they didn't talk much about their old
life. He guessed they must have been pretty well
off in Vietnam, for they were educated and had
good jobs.

He was the last of his siblings to go off to college.
When he took a course in late twentieth-century
conflict, which was mostly about the war in
Vietnam, he learned how much his people had
suffered.

He went home to his parents angry, but they said
he could spend the rest of his life mourning over
something he never knew...or make something
out of what he had been given.

JOB 38:12-13

"Have you commanded the morning
     since your days began,
   and caused the dawn to know its
        place,
so that it might take hold of the skirts of
     the earth,
   and the wicked be shaken out of it?"

The Cleaners

She took his clothes without looking at him. "What do you have?" She spoke the words in an accent so thick he could barely understand her.

"A suit," he said.

"Thursday okay?" she asked, studying the computer terminal that doubled as a cash register.

"Sure," he said.

She handed him his receipt without a word. The exchange had lasted less than a minute.

As he reached for the doorknob, he turned on impulse and smiled. "Thank you," he said. "I really appreciate your help."

She looked up at him for the first time and returned his smile.

Isaiah 58:8

> Then your light shall break forth
>   like the dawn,
>   and your healing shall spring up
>   quickly;
> your vindicator shall go before you,
>   the glory of the Lord shall be
>   your rear guard.

Unrelenting Love

She had her mother's eyes and her mother's small voice, but the rest came from the father she had never met.

The girl was sixteen when she heard the full story from her mother. A dinner date and a one-night fling, loveless but not passionless, had been her conception. The love had come later, when her mother chose to keep her and live for her. She had never known her mother to even look at another man.

It was hard being the meaning of someone else's life. Sometimes she wished her mother would find another interest to divert her unceasing care.

Her mother's love was the way she imagined God's love to be—and why, she supposed, some people need to run away from God.

Psalm 139:7

Where can I go from your spirit?
  Or where can I flee from your presence?

Dinner Game

It was a dinner game the father loved to play. He would throw out a profusion of off-beat questions for his kids to answer. "What is your favorite color?" "What season do you like best?" "What is your favorite TV show?"

The final question was always the same, however: "When you meet God eye-to-eye, what words do you hope to hear?"

It was as if he was searching through all their answers to hear what God might say to him.

Matthew 25:34

> "Then the king will say to those at his right hand, 'Come, you that are blessed by my Father, inherit the kingdom prepared for you from the foundation of the world.'"

DEADLY ALTERNATIVE

"You're being punished," said his friend, "because you can't say no to anyone."

"That doesn't make sense," he responded. "Why should I be punished for being good to people?"

"It's not really punishment. You're a good man. People count on you," his friend responded, realizing that behind this mock whining were real feelings of being used.

"But I don't want to be counted on. I want to be left alone," the man continued.

"Face it," his friend said, "if you were left alone, if no one turned to you, what would your life be like?"

"Peaceful," came the reply.

"No," said his friend, "deadly."

SIRACH 7:33

Give graciously to all the living;
do not withhold kindness even
from the dead.

THE PURPOSE OF ANGELS

"I'm glad there are angels," the woman said to her neighbor over coffee.

"Angels?" Her friend looked at her with raised eyebrows. "What made you think about angels?"

"Well," she said, "I was thinking how often I just forget about God, how I go through whole days without even the tiniest thought of God—and I don't think I'm the only one."

Her friend rolled her eyes.

The woman continued, "If I'm not paying attention to God and other people aren't either, that's where angels come in. They can spend a whole day thinking about God while we're busy."

"So angels are supposed to do our praying for us?" the friend asked incredulously.

REVELATION 5:11

Then I looked, and I heard the voice
of many angels surrounding the
throne and the living creatures and
the elders; they numbered myriads of
myriads and thousands of thousands.

ONE MOMENT OF PEACE

Just home from the hospital, their baby son Jonah lay on the old beat-up couch in the living room. Two-year-old Lucas sat eating cut-up hot dogs and creamed corn—a specialty his father had concocted for him. The family was wrapped the peace of the moment.

Without provocation or warning, Lucas threw his fork across the room and started screaming. Then Jonah began to scream. Their idyllic scene of peace had ended—which was all right...as long as they could all remember later what the moment had been like.

JOHN 14:27

"Peace I leave with you; my peace I give to you. I do not give to you as the world gives."

BITS OF CREATION

Born with Down's Syndrome, he struggled with many of the details of a baffling world.

Raking leaves one morning, he sat on the cold October ground and studied each leaf, turning it over and over, counting the veins, marveling at the colors, before putting it on a pile.

He who rarely saw the big picture of things retained the gift of noting and approving the tiniest bits of creation.

MATTHEW 11:25

At that time Jesus said, "I thank you, Father, Lord of heaven and earth, because you have hidden these things from the wise and the intelligent and have revealed them to infants."

THIS OLD HOUSE

The day got off to a bad start when the plumbers showed up at 7:30 in the morning to work on the plugged tub drain. They were altogether too cheery for his taste, announcing as they tramped up the stairs in their waterproof boots, "Old houses are great to live in but a pain to keep up. Of course, they keep us in business."

Two hours later they came to him in his study. "Like God might say about creation, we've got good news and bad news," they told him. "The good news is, we know what's plugging up the drain. The bad news is, it can't be fixed right until you redo the plumbing. It'll work okay for the most part, but until you can start all over, you'll just have to work with what you've got."

MATTHEW 7:24

"Everyone then who hears these words of mine and acts on them will be like a wise man who built his house on rock."

The Right Clothes

That Sunday's gospel was about the king who threw a wedding banquet and no one came. The king sent his servants out to haul in total strangers, good as well as bad. Finally, he threw out one poor fellow because he wasn't wearing the right clothes. After the reading, the priest pointed to a young man in ragged shorts and a tank top and said: "You heard Jesus. Out!"

The young man was startled but got up and walked out.

It was so quiet in the church people heard the candles sputtering. Jesus couldn't possibly have meant this story to be interpreted in this way.

After Mass, the priest was seen giving the young man high fives, and people realized that they had just witnessed a very effective homily.

Luke 10:23-24

> Then turning to the disciples, Jesus said to them privately: "Blessed are the eyes that see what you see! For I tell you that many prophets and kings desired to see what you see, but did not see it, and to hear what you hear, but did not hear it."

THE CHAIN LETTER

It hadn't occurred to her that chain letters could be sent by e-mail until she got one. She read it because it began with a joke about a young priest who drank too much vodka before preaching to calm himself down and then got everything all mixed up. Then she read the little note at the bottom that said: "This is a chain letter. It will bring you good luck if you pass it on to twelve people, bad if you trash it." Her stomach became queasy. She wasn't supposed to use the company e-mail for personal messages. She didn't have a computer at home. But she couldn't afford any more bad luck.

Then a coworker reminded her that getting through each day is not a matter of luck, good or bad, but of faithfulness to what you really believe.

So she pushed the delete button.

PSALM 97:11

Light dawns for the righteous,
    and joy for the upright in heart.

Choose Goodness

Shopping for Halloween costumes with her children, she was dismayed when they were drawn to the most outlandish, most awful of the lot. "Don't you want to be a princess?" she asked her daughter. "Don't you want to be a knight?" she said to her son. "How about matching pumpkins with big smiling faces?" she said to both.

"But Halloween is supposed to be scary," said her son. "Yea," agreed her daughter.

"But you're not scary," she said to them.

"But we could be," said her son. "Yea," agreed her daughter.

"Yes," she said to them both, "I guess we all can be whatever we choose to be."

She gave in then, admitting that scariness is a choice—just like goodness.

DEUTERONOMY 30:19

> I have set before you life and death,
> blessings and curses. Choose life so that
> you and your descendants may live.

TRICK OR TREAT?

On the day before Halloween, his friend asked if he'd bought treats for the children who would to come to the door of his new house. He looked amazed; he hadn't thought about Halloween since he was a kid. No one ever knocked on the apartment door where he used to live.

"I don't have anything and I'm not sure I will," he said.

"But it's Halloween," his friend insisted. "The children will be disappointed—and they just might vandalize your home."

"They wouldn't," he said, but on the way home, he stopped at a grocery store to buy several bags of candy.

On Halloween night, as the children came to his door, he was not as annoyed as he thought he would be.

MARK 10:14

"Let the little children come to me; do not stop them; for it is to such as these that the kingdom of God belongs."

THE TRAIL GUIDE

She had not thought about her volunteer work as a trail guide at the state park as a spiritual choice. Not, that is, until the day a tiny child asked her, "Do all these birds and trees belong to you?"

PSALM 8:6

You have given them dominion over the
works of your hands;
you have put all things under their feet.

THE COMMUNITY

They sat in a long semicircle around the convent community room. The recitation of their names was like a medieval litany: Aquinas, Thomasine, Chrysostom, Alphonsus, Luke, Gregory, Leonis, Justin, Athanasia. Years ago, at their professions, these women had taken as their own the names of great men. Now, in their old age the irony was not lost on them: it was they who kept the memory of these great men alive by living simple lives.

REVELATION 7:14

These are they who have come out of the great ordeal; they have washed their robes and made them white in the blood of the Lamb.

Traveling Clothes

She had picked out the dress she wanted to be buried in, a bright pink one with subtle embroidery around the neck. She included undergarments, a pair of beige shoes, and her favorite pearl necklace and earrings. All these items she wrapped in tissue paper and packed in a suitcase labeled "Traveling clothes" and subtitled "Mom's burial clothes." It was light against the years of gentle kindness that would wrap her soul on the journey.

Revelation 14:13

> "Yes," says the Spirit, "they will rest from their labors, for their deeds follow them."

COWARDS

There are no cowards in the kingdom of God.
Unless, of course, you count all the women and
men who were seized by grace against their better
judgment and who may have surprised themselves and others . . . but not God.

2 THESSALONIANS 1:11

Our God will make you worthy of his
call and will fulfill by his power every
good resolve and work of faith.

The Calling

Everyone keeps telling him he should be a priest. He doesn't want to hear it anymore. He doesn't care if they think he's gifted, just the right sort to preside at the community's common table, good with people and even better at presenting a credible gospel witness. He doesn't need the pressure. He wants God to let him off the hook or give him a clear, irrevocable sign that this is what he's supposed to do with his life.

Romans 11:29

> For the gifts and the calling of God are irrevocable.

APPLE JUICE

It could only happen in second grade. Standing for morning prayers, the little girl noticed that the boy next to her was trembling and then she saw why. A puddle had formed at his feet and a dark spot down the front of his pants.

As the prayer ended, she lifted up her desk top and took out her lunch—which just happened to have a big cup of apple juice in it. Somehow the apple juice spilled all over the boy next to her, down his front and onto the floor. The other children laughed at her and made fun of her clumsiness.

PHILIPPIANS 2:4

Let each of you look not to your own interests, but to the interests of others.

SMALL MIRACLE

As a couple, they are not as strong as they used to be. He can barely walk. At the grocery store, he sits in the car while she shops. Last week, she left her purse in the shopping cart. They were halfway across town before she realized it. When they got back, they discovered that one of the teenagers who usually frightened them so had found her purse and turned it in.

PHILIPPIANS 2:14-15

Do all things without murmuring and arguing, so that you may be blameless and innocent, children of God without blemish in the midst of a crooked and perverse generation, in which you shine like stars in the world.

BUSY SIGNAL

When he was a kid and they still said Mass in Latin, he used to get bored in church. He'd kneel in the front row, take out his rosary, and carefully scratch his name into the old wood of the pew. Sister caught him and led him to the back of the church.

"Jesus is trying to talk to you," she said, "and you're not listening."

"I listened," the boy said, "but he was busy talking to Father."

Sister smiled and said: "You're old enough to wait your turn patiently."

That's how he learned to wait his turn with God—and God always got around to him in time.

ROMANS 14:12

So then, each of us will be accountable to God.

Final Payment

He never learned to use anything with a handle: rake, shovel, hoe, hammer, frying pan, or lawn mower. He simply quit working altogether when he was about twenty-four. He had big ideas and handed out lots of advice, but his ideas never panned out and his advice usually turned sour.

At seventy, he surprised everyone in the neighborhood by mounting a newly-purchased riding snow blower and cleaning the driveways and sidewalks of the whole block. It was one great burst of energy and benevolence that earned him a generous collective memory after he died—three days later.

Romans 15:14

> I myself feel confident about you, my brothers and sisters, that you yourselves are full of goodness.

Lingering Grief

Three of her friends died this year. She wrote a mutual friend: "There is so much unresolved with these deaths. I would have liked more time to say the things I needed to say. When Jesus comes again, will he wipe out the memory of these things, or will I finally be able to forgive?"

Her friend wrote back: "It's possible that we will be able to forgive people in heaven, but can we explain why their grievances have lingered so long in our hearts?"

Philippians 3:20-21

But our citizenship is in heaven, and it is from there that we are expecting a Savior, the Lord Jesus Christ. He will transform the body of our humiliation that it may be conformed to the body of his glory.

Surprise Announcement

Her parents had been less than solicitous about her welfare when she was growing up. In the end, she had turned out fine, avoiding the pitfalls of adolescence in a post-modern world and keeping her faith in an anti-Christian society. She was independent and determined. She had put herself through college and then married well.

When her first child was born, she had sent a birth announcement to her parents. Her mother called her in surprise. "We didn't even know you were pregnant," she said. "Why didn't you tell you us?"

"You never seemed that interested," she replied.

Her mother paused and then said, "I didn't know you wanted my interest."

Philippians 4:10

I rejoice in the Lord greatly that now at last you have revived your concern for me; indeed, you were concerned for me, but had no opportunity to show it.

THE QUESTION

After sitting through several weeks of religious education class, one tenth grader raised her hand and asked, "Tell me again why I should even believe in God?"

The old priest was no longer shocked by questions like this. They were a sign of the times and of a society that no longer just takes it for granted that God exists.

"Young lady," he said, "I cannot prove that God exists, and I do not think I can convince you that God loves you. I do believe you can discover both truths. If I could I would give you my faith, but I cannot. I can only give you what you and I can discover together."

WISDOM 1:1-2

Think of the Lord in goodness
and seek him with sincerity of heart;
because he is found by those who do
     not put him to the test,
and manifests himself to those who do
     not distrust him.

INVINCIBLE

The winds came barreling in out of the north and he pulled his coat more tightly around him. There was a time when the cold would not have bothered him, when he believed he was invincible and could withstand anything. It was not until his sense of invulnerability left him in old age that he learned there was something more secure than his own powers and proclivities.

LUKE 17:5

The apostles said to the Lord, "Increase our faith!"

ETERNITY

He was riding his bike home from school when he knew, just knew somehow, that his brother had died. There was no out-of-body experience, no angel wings flapping above his head, no apparition, just the sure and steady knowledge that his brother no longer waited for him at home—but was waiting for him in eternity.

MATTHEW 13:43

"Then the righteous will shine like the sun in the kingdom of their Father."

THE BREAKUP

He wanted to say there was no point in continuing the relationship. He had tried to adapt to her changing needs and demands, but each adaptation seemed to inspire more expectations. It was a vicious game he no longer wanted to play.

She pouted when he told her. She said if he was any kind of a man he wouldn't be deserting her when she needed him most.

He wondered how they had gotten this far...and if there were any way they could ever return to the love they once knew.

COLOSSIANS 3:13-15

> Bear with one another and, if anyone has a complaint against another, forgive each other; just as the Lord has forgiven you, so you also must forgive. Above all, clothe yourselves with love, which binds everything together in perfect harmony. And let the peace of Christ rule in your hearts.

Between Two Worlds

When the changes of Vatican II were taking place, she was thoughtfully ignorant of their importance. She prayed as she had always prayed: in back of the church, in the dark, a rosary in one hand and a Latin/English missal in the other.

When they renovated her church and eliminated the dark corners and most of the statues, nothing in her prayer changed. She didn't need statues and darkness to find God.

When they took out the nation's and the papal flags, however, she was oddly disturbed. She told a friend, "The flags always reminded me that we are caught between this world and the next."

Titus 3:1-2

Remind them to be subject to rulers and authorities, to be obedient, to be ready for every good work, to speak evil of no one, to avoid quarreling, to be gentle, and to show every courtesy to everyone.

THE HEART OF A SAINT

He had been a bishop for twenty years. After he retired, he visited those who were dying from AIDS every day. He brought them communion, prayed with them, and offered them his firm hand to hold. He always seemed so strong, sure that God was near.

After his death, a longtime admirer said, "When he was around, you just knew there was a purpose to our lives and that we'd all get home to God one way or another."

PHILEMON 1:7

I have indeed received much joy and encouragement from your love, because the hearts of the saints have been refreshed through you, my brother.

BEAUTY

The two of them went for a long walk that cold night. Neither said much, both were lost in the horizons of their own speculations. Finally one of them spoke: "Do you suppose there is life on other planets?"

His friend replied, "There is life wherever God is, I suppose, and God is everywhere tonight."

WISDOM 13:3

If through delight in the beauty of these
    things people assumed them to be gods,
let them know how much better than these
    is their Lord,
for the author of beauty created them.

Woolly Lambs

She didn't know when the collection started. Maybe it was old toys from her five children that began the woolly assembly. Maybe it was a cuddly toy she purchased for her classroom that never made it to school. Whatever the origins, she now had more stuffed lambs than anyone else she knew. When she was asked, "Why lambs?" she had no good answer.

"I believe it has something to do with Jesus," she said. "I only know that they make me smile and I am always comforted by their presence."

John 1:29
___

The next day he saw Jesus coming toward him and declared, "Here is the Lamb of God who takes away the sin of the world!"

HEAVEN'S DANCE

If he had a great sadness, it was that he never learned to dance. Dancing seemed to reveal a kind of freedom of spirit that always eluded him. He had to believe that if they gave dance lessons in heaven, no one would snicker if you stepped on your partner's feet. Maybe that is the beauty of heaven: angels don't have feet—or egos—to stub.

1 JOHN 4:16-17

God is love and those who abide in love abide in God, and God abides in them. Love has been perfected among us in this: that we may have boldness on the day of judgment, because as he is, so are we in this world.

Examination of Conscience

When he was twenty-two, he told his pastor in confession that he liked to examine his conscience every day to make sure he was on the right track. His pastor, rightfully afraid he might become scrupulous, cautioned against too much self-reflection. "Once a week might be enough," the pastor had counseled. After a while, even that seemed too often, so the man stopped the practice altogether.

Now, at fifty-two, he is as successful and happy as one can get. Only one thing bothers him—the nagging thought that he is missing something very important.

Revelation 2:5

Remember then from what you have
fallen; repent, and do the works you
did at first.

Hero

It's hard to be a hero when no one expects anything from you.

John 14:12

"Very truly, I tell you, the one who believes in me will also do the works that I do and, in fact, will do greater works than these."

THE "ORPHANS' FEAST"

The two of them made a pact during the first year of their marriage that they would never eat Thanksgiving dinner alone in their home. Each year, they would search out people who were far away from family and host an "orphans' feast." Each year, new people came. Occasionally, a stranger who had heard about their hospitality would knock on the door just in time for pie and coffee.

REVELATION 3:20

> "Listen! I am standing at the door, knocking; if you hear my voice and open the door, I will come in to you and eat with you, and you with me."

In His Arms

When she was a little girl, she used to fall asleep on her father's lap during Mass. One Sunday evening when she was in college she attended a late liturgy at the campus parish. Kneeling through the Eucharistic Prayer she prayed intently for her father, who had died the previous year. She slouched back against her pew, laid her head on her arms, and fell asleep. Someone nudged her when it was time for communion.

Psalm 17:8

Guard me as the apple of the eye;
   hide me in the shadow of your wings.

THE FLIGHT

The older couple walked into church with their youngest daughter, her small son dragging along behind them. It had been less than a year since her divorce, and her parents knew that this visit was a flight from memories not yet healed. When the final blessing came, her father put his arm around her, lifted her son onto his shoulders, and led the parade out of the church.

3 JOHN 1:5-6

> You will do well to send them on in a manner worthy of God; for they began their journey for the sake of Christ, accepting no support from non-believers. Therefore we ought to support such people, so that we may become co-workers with the truth.

Tough Love

Six months ago, his parents had asked him to leave. At twenty-four years old, they said, it was time for him to be on his own. He moved from their house to his girlfriend's apartment. Most of his clothes are still in plastic garbage bags in the back seat of his car. Stuffed in the glove compartment is a stack of envelopes from the State of Wisconsin informing him of the revocation of his driver's license for nonpayment of fines.

The day before Thanksgiving, his father called to invite him to come with them to church and then join them for dinner.

"God," the young man replied sarcastically, "is an idea made up for people who can't manage their lives. What time is dinner?"

His father, with the patience of the illusory God said, "One o'clock."

MATTHEW 7:11

"If you then . . . know how to give good gifts to your children, how much more will your Father in heaven give good things to those who ask him!"

HOME FOR THE HOLIDAYS

He drove to his parents' home for Thanksgiving
dinner. Although he had never been especially
close to them, there was still a strong pull for him
to go back to his beginnings. He hoped that the
same kind of primal tug would eventually draw him
back to God, his other beginning.

LUKE 15:20

"So he set off and went to his father.
But while he was still far off, his father
saw him and was filled with compassion; he ran and put his arm around
him and kissed him."

LABOR OF LOVE

She knew, even as she rose early to put the turkey in the oven and begin the other preparations for dinner, that this would be the last time she would cook such a meal for her family. The doctor had told her that she had only weeks to live.

She peeled potatoes, whipped cream, opened the corn, slid the cranberries out onto her grandmother's relish dish, and cut celery into sticks for dipping. By eleven she was exhausted, but everything was ready.

LUKE 21:4

"She out of her poverty has
put in all she had to live on."

Weeds and Wheat

On a Tuesday morning she was riding the train to work and suddenly realized that she had never planted a thing—not a vegetable garden, not a flower box, not even a single seed. She wondered if she would be weed or wheat in heaven's garden...and if God liked the smell of dandelions as much as lilies.

Matthew 6:28-29

"Consider the lilies of the field, how they grow; they neither toil nor spin, yet I tell you, even Solomon in all his glory was not clothed like one of these."

Earthquake

On the way to work, he was listening to the news about the California earthquake. He stopped at a red light and suddenly felt the earth rumble beneath his car.

"We don't have earthquakes in Minnesota," he said aloud to calm himself. Then he saw the large crane across the street retract a wrecking ball from a pile of rubble. Meanwhile, he hadn't noticed that the light had turned green. The driver of the car behind him pulled ahead and bumped into him. For the second time that day he felt the earth move.

"Perhaps God is trying to tell me something," he thought.

1 Kings 19:11

Now there was a great wind, so strong that it was splitting mountains and breaking rocks in pieces before the Lord, but the Lord was not in the wind; and after the wind an earthquake, but the Lord was not in the earthquake.

Every Perfect Gift

She lived on a tight budget and there was little to spare. Outside the bank where she had just cashed her paycheck, a panhandler begged for money. "Clever," she thought to herself. "If you're going to beg for money, you might as well do it where there's plenty of it."

She threw two quarters into his hat and then she stopped and made a quick visit to church.

James 1:17

Every generous act of giving, with every perfect gift, is from above, coming down from the Father of lights, with whom there is no variation or shadow due to change.

THE BATTLE

It was a typical morning. Their daughter had commandeered the bathroom first and was curling her hair while her two brothers banged on the door, demanding entry. By the time they all made it down to breakfast each had taken a defensive position (which they knew in their hearts was offensive). The sniping continued through juice pouring. Finally, as their mother poured cereal into their bowls, she declared a truce (which she knew in her heart would not lead to peace).

ISAIAH 2:4

They shall beat their swords into
    plowshares,
  and their spears into pruning hooks;
nation shall not lift up sword against
    nation,
    neither shall they learn war any more.

SHELTER

She adapted easily to the warm and sunny winters of Tucson. She had waited all her working life to get away from the cold northern winters and would not apologize for her flight to warmth. But she did pray every night for those who had no warm place to sleep, and she wrote regular checks to a homeless shelter back in Milwaukee. It was a sign to God that her heart was in the right place, even if her body wasn't.

ISAIAH 4:5-6

Indeed over all the glory there will be a canopy. It will serve as a pavilion, a shade by day from the heat, and a refuge and shelter from the storm and rain.

END TIMES

God, in the days to come,

when Christ leaves your right side

and rides the clouds for the last time;

when the rumors you circulated,

about women in labor crying out

and mothers' milk drying up, come true;

will you, as you promised,

keep your eyes open?

ISAIAH 30:19

Truly, O people in Zion, inhabitants
of Jerusalem, you shall weep no
more. He will surely be gracious to
you at the sound of your cry; when
he hears it, he will answer you.

GOD'S CIRCLE

God, in those days,

when your voice crosses the sound barrier

and trumpets like thunder in every ear;

when we are caught dancing,

winding bonds 'round each other

that pass as drunkenness

and fall dizzy before your truth;

will you, as you have promised,

stand in our circle?

ISAIAH 7:18-19

> On that day the Lord will whistle for
> the fly that is at the sources of the
> streams of Egypt, and for the bee that
> is in the land of Assyria. And they
> will all come and settle in the steep
> ravines, and in the clefts of the rocks,
> and on all the thorn bushes, and on
> all the pastures.

Prayer and Promise

And God, when, as you say he must,

Christ takes the judgment seat;

and when our futures,

held together by prayer and promise,

story and song,

fall from our hands;

will you, as we hope,

raise your right hand

and bring to a good end

what you have begun?

Isaiah 4:2

On that day the branch of the
Lord shall be beautiful and
glorious, and the fruit of the land
shall be the pride and glory of the
survivors of Israel.

Advent Quiz

This year they were going to teach their children the true meaning of Christmas. During the first week of Advent, they sat them down and quizzed them.

"What happened on the first Christmas?" they asked.

The children answered, "Jesus was born."

"Why do people put bright lights on trees?" they asked.

The children answered, "Because Jesus is the light of the world."

"Why do we give gifts at Christmas?" they asked.

The children answered, "So we can get new toys."

Oh, well, two out of three ain't bad!

Isaiah 29:23

> For when he sees his children;
>   the work of my hands, in his midst,
>   they will sanctify my name.

CHRISTMAS LIST

She vowed that this year she would get her
Christmas shopping done early. On the first
Saturday, she sat down to make out her list. She
wrote down the names of everyone for whom she
intended to get a gift and a dash next to each
name. Then she just sat drinking tea.

There was nothing any of these people *needed*
that she could buy them.

The things they *needed* were not for sale at any
price.

MATTHEW 13: 45-46

"Again, the kingdom of heaven
is like a merchant in search of
fine pearls; on finding one pearl
of great value, he went and sold
all that he had and bought it."

Voice of Conscience

She didn't believe people had consciences. She believed instead that some people were born without the ability to do anything really bad, while most people simply made their way in this world. If that meant stealing to feed their families, that's just the way it was. If that meant lying to get a better job, that's just the way it was. If that meant slugging someone over the head at the automated teller to get cash to buy drugs, that's just the way it was.

This view made her world less complicated...but not more grace-filled.

Isaiah 30:21
___

> And when you turn to the right or
> when you turn to the left, your ears
> shall hear a word behind you, saying,
> "This is the way; walk in it."

LEFT-HANDED LOVE

She pulled into her driveway and forgot to put on the parking brake before she got out to open the garage door. The surprise of its backward roll on the slight incline caught her between getting in and out of the car. Her left foot slipped on an icy patch and she tumbled out of the car. Her right arm was crushed beneath the left front wheel.

Recovery took a long time, and she prayed a lot. She'd always enjoyed easy conversations with God, but their relationship became strained as her impatience for recovery grew.

One day, over a year later, it was time to write out Christmas cards. Her writing hand was useless. Pulling herself straight up in her chair, she closed her eyes and looked straight at God. "Okay, God, what am I supposed to do now?" she asked. At that moment one of her grandnephews walked in with a new typewriter, an early Christmas present from the family. "Isn't this great, Auntie?" he said, "You can type out little notes to everyone with your left hand."

Every card she sent that year was signed: "With all my left-handed love."

ISAIAH 30:26

The LORD binds up the injuries
of his people, and heals the
wounds inflicted by his blow.

Absent-Minded Professor

He was wonderful, witty, entertaining, bright, and kind, but he was incompetent at doing basic everyday things—the original absent-minded professor. People said it was because he had lived in institutions since he was thirteen. He'd never had to do his own laundry, never had to cook or keep a budget.

His friends took over the everyday tasks for him. They made sure he had clean underwear and went out and bought new clothes when he ran low. They left meals in his refrigerator or freezer with explicit instructions—then they would call and guide him through the actual preparation. They even balanced his checkbook for him.

Some people were irritated by the way others looked out for him. Of course these were not his friends; they were people who peeked in on the lives of others.

John 15:15

"I do not call you servants any longer, because the servant does not know what the master is doing; but I have called you friends, because I have made known to you everything that I have heard from my Father."

Home for the Holidays

When her parents sent her plane tickets home for Christmas it wasn't just because they missed her. It was because she hadn't spoken to her brother in over ten years. They didn't tell her he would be there.

And the ransomed of the LORD shall return,
    and come to Zion with singing;
everlasting joy shall be upon their heads;
    they shall obtain joy and gladness,
    and sorrow and sighing shall flee away.

GOD'S MEMORY

You are God's memory in this world.

Stand up! Look around you. See.

Your friends and neighbors and children,

all look to you as a sign of God's justice,

as the hope of the future,

as one who does not forget them.

ISAIAH 40:3

A voice cries out:
"In the wilderness prepare the way of
    the LORD,
  make straight in the desert a highway
    for our God."

FADED BEAUTY

"Why is it," she wondered as she rummaged through her boxes of Christmas decorations, "that tinsel and glitter and silk poinsettias fade by the second Christmas, but old nativity scenes retain their beauty for generations?"

ISAIAH 40:8

The grass withers, the flower fades;
 but the word of our God will stand
 forever.

Too Busy

She told herself she was too busy to pray:
"There's just too much to do to get ready for
Christmas."

Psalm 80:14-15

Turn again, O God of hosts;
  look down from heaven, and see;
have regard for this vine,
  the stock that your right hand has planted.

CHRISTMAS CARDS

He reached across the table for yet another
Christmas card. He had been writing them for
several hours. He wished Christmas was over
already so he could get back to his real life.

JOHN 1:1-3

In the beginning was the Word, and
the Word was with God, and the
Word was God. He was in the
beginning with God. All things came
into being through him, and without
him not one thing came into being.

THE MESSENGER

At eighty years old, she was the first one to Mass every day. The pastor eventually gave her a key and asked her to open up every morning; it gave him five extra minutes of sleep.

One year a huge early December snow storm hit the city. The pastor took one look out the window and decided no one would come to church that morning and went back to sleep. Thirty minutes later, there was a banging at the rectory door. He went down in slippers and bathrobe, and there she was.

"I'm here and I've already lit the Advent candles," she said commandingly, "now get on some clothes and let's have Mass."

ZEPHANIAH 3:12

> For I will leave in the midst of you
> a people humble and lowly.
> They shall seek refuge in the name of
> the LORD.

Blinded to the Light

Every city has someone who puts up countless strings of Christmas lights and dazzling displays, with floodlights so bright they hurt your eyes. Their houses make it on the local news and wreak havoc in the neighborhood as gawkers clog the streets.

There is a difference between celebrating and showing off.

Isaiah 45:7

I form light and create darkness,
I make weal and create woe;
I the Lord do all these things.

HOLDING GOD

How do you hold something, not because you're afraid you're going to break it but because it's important?

How do you hold something, not because it's going to slip through your fingers but because you can't live without it?

How do you hold something as final as a loved one's last breath or as passionate as a lover's first kiss?

How do you hold God?

MATTHEW 1:19-20

Her husband Joseph, being a righteous man and unwilling to expose her to public disgrace, planned to dismiss her quietly. But just when he had resolved to do this, an angel of the Lord appeared to him in a dream and said, "Joseph, son of David, do not be afraid to take Mary as your wife, for the child conceived in her is from the Holy Spirit."

EXPECTATIONS

In our curious way, we never quite understand our expectations: the distance between what we wanted and what we sought; between what we sought and what we chose; between what we chose and what we got; and, even more, between what we were given and what we deserved.

LUKE 1:13

But the angel said to him, "Do not be afraid, Zechariah, for your prayer has been heard. Your wife Elizabeth will bear you a son, and you will name him John."

THE RIDDLE

Isn't this the riddle of Christmas: that we would be God and God would be us?

LUKE 1:26-27

In the sixth month the angel Gabriel was sent by God to a town in Galilee called Nazareth, to a virgin engaged to a man whose name was Joseph, of the house of David. The virgin's name was Mary.

Anger, Fear, Hope

We are known by our anger, our fear, and our hope.

The anger that is deliberate, and comforting, that strikes the turned cheek and leaves us tired and depressed.

The fear that sinks into our souls and surprises us with its power, that makes us leap to conclusions and discover the margins of our prejudice.

The hope that rides our shoulders in hospital waiting rooms, that bends our memories as we attempt to recapture our childhoods.

Luke 1:39-40

In those days Mary set out and went with haste to a Judean town in the hill country, where she entered the house of Zechariah and greeted Elizabeth.

Mary's Grace

Mary was too old for childish games and too young for seduction when she heard the voice of grace in her own assent: "Let it be." What must it be like to face the future knowing that God is no longer "out there"?

Luke 1:46-47

"My soul magnifies the Lord,
and my spirit rejoices in God my
Savior."

Silence

In a world where hope is hard to come by, we often mistake silence for bated breath.

Luke 1:63-64

[Zechariah] asked for a writing tablet and wrote, "His name is John." And all of them were amazed. Immediately his mouth was opened and his tongue freed, and he began to speak, praising God.

THE PEOPLE

Always the story begins with people.

And there are no illusions about us.

Wandering in darkness—that's us,

face to face with ourselves,

looking into the mirror of starless nights,

pacing the floor when we can't sleep,

lost in our own thoughts,

stumbling over words

which never say all we want to say,

but sometimes say too much.

ISAIAH 9:2

The people who walked in darkness
    have seen a great light;
those who lived in a land of deep
    darkness–
    on them light has shined.

MEETING GOD

When we, beset by a season of good cheer, come to this day, swallowing Christmas like wine after a wordy toast, catching ourselves in the breach between believing and unbelieving, suspicion and indifference, do we look to meet God for the first time—or once again?

LUKE 2:8-12

In that region there were shepherds living in the fields, keeping watch over their flock by night. Then an angel of the Lord stood before them, and the glory of the Lord shone around them, and they were terrified. But the angel said to them, "Do not be afraid; for see—I am bringing you good news of great joy for all the people: to you is born this day in the city of David a Savior, who is the Messiah, the Lord. This will be a sign for you: you will find a child wrapped in bands of cloth and lying in a manger."

Salt of Our Tears

We love oddly, and this is our bond with God and Christmas.

For surely, never quite understanding the course of our own affections, we can sympathize with the God who, we are told, dreamed of us, sought us, chose us, who will not relinquish one of our smiles to the clutter of the past, and who remembers feeling the salt of our tears in his wounds.

Hebrews 1:1-2

Long ago God spoke to our ancestors in many and various ways by the prophets, but in these last days he has spoken to us by a Son, whom he appointed heir of all things, through whom he also created the worlds.

HANDS

These hands . . .

touched and not touched,

scarred by a thousand mistakes,

rough as determination,

soft as negligence,

careful as hesitation,

hard as divorce,

holy as an alcoholic's last drink.

These hands, we say, have held God.

---

1 JOHN 1:1-2

We declare to you what was from the beginning, what we have heard, what we have seen with our eyes, what we have looked at and touched with our hands, concerning the word of life— this life was revealed, and we have seen it and testify to it.

THE FIRST MARTYRS

The first martyrs were too young to understand that belief and unbelief are both costly.

MATTHEW 2:16

> When Herod saw that he had been
> tricked by the wise men, he was
> infuriated, and he sent and killed all
> the children in and around
> Bethlehem who were two years old or
> under, according to the time that he
> had learned from the wise men.

THE TANGERINES

She stood at the grocery store checkout counter with her three children. The checkout boy slid things along quickly, finally weighing her tangerines and totaling the bill. It was just under ten dollars. The woman pulled a single ten dollar bill from her purse and paused, looking quickly at her three children. "Excuse me," she said quietly, "I think you punched in oranges instead of tangerines."

"You're right," the boy responded, replacing the tangerines on the scale and punching in a new code. Totaling the new bill he said, "That'll be $10.17."

The woman looked at her ten dollar bill and then down at the tangerines. She picked up the bag and pulled out one tangerine. "Could you re-total it please?" she asked calmly and without bowing her head.

LUKE 2:22, 24

They brought him up to Jerusalem to present him to the Lord . . . and they offered a sacrifice according to what is stated in the law of the Lord, "a pair of turtledoves or two young pigeons."

Something Special

There was something special about her. Everyone who knew her well recognized it as an interior goodness that shone in all she said and did. New acquaintances just remarked on her nice smile and gentle eyes.

Luke 2:40

The child grew and became strong, filled with wisdom; and the favor of God was upon him.

HOPE OF THIS AGE

You who bear the weight of the world,

who know the burdens of work and worry,

who carry anxiety and need in your purse,

stand up straight, bear yourself honorably,

for you are marked by God to be just,

to be the hope of this age.

1 JOHN 2:18

Children, it is the last hour!